It's Not Harder Than Cancer

*The Mindsets You Need to Survive and Thrive
After Serious Illness*

By Michael Holtz

ISBN-13: 978-1514307786

Dedications

For Sarah, my love, my wife, my life's partner and the world's best caregiver. Thank you for taking care of me and saving my life

For Zane, my superhero friend, encourager and cheerleader. Thank you for helping me find a new life after illness.

For Reece, my father-in-law, who wanted this book written as much as I did. Thank you for believing.

Contents

Foreword

Kevin Conroy
Chairman and Chief Executive Officer
Exact Sciences Corp.
Madison, Wisconsin

Michael Holtz is the kind of man who can bring a ballroom full of people to tears and have them laughing a few moments later. He is a survivor and an inspiration to the millions of people who have been impacted by colorectal cancer. I first met Michael when he spoke to the team here at Exact Sciences. We were on the verge of receiving FDA approval for Cologuard, our innovative, noninvasive, DNA-based colorectal cancer screening test. We were meeting to train nearly 100 new team members who would go out and talk to physicians about the importance of getting their patients screened and about Cologuard, a new weapon in the fight against this second most deadly cancer. Educating physicians about Cologuard wasn't going to be easy, and it would be a test for this group of young professionals. As a team, we knew the statistics: colorectal cancer is preventable if caught early, and screening can save lives. But more than statistics, our team needed to understand what it feels like to be impacted by colorectal cancer, what it means to fight the fight.

Michael shared the details of his own battle with rectal cancer. He told us how he had just completed a marathon and was in the best shape of his life when he found out he was sick. He was young and healthy: it was proof that colorectal cancer doesn't discriminate. It is a terrible disease that can impact anyone. He shared with our team the gratitude he felt toward his family and friends, the people who supported him and helped him fight. He used his humor and charisma to reach everyone in the audience.

More than 136,000 people will be diagnosed with colorectal cancer in the U.S. this year alone, and more than 50,000 people will die as a result of this terrible disease. These statistics don't have to stand: we can win the fight against colorectal cancer. It is often referred to as the most preventable but least prevented cancer. We know that screening can catch the disease early, in some cases before it even becomes cancer. This is a fact that more people need to hear if we want to defeat colorectal cancer. Brave warriors like Michael who share their stories and encourage people to take control of their own health are critical in this fight, and the combination of their passion and scientific advances like Cologuard will be necessary for us to defeat colorectal cancer.

When we started our company meeting I had asked the new team members to stand up if they knew someone who had been touched by colorectal cancer. A few stood up. The morning after Michael spoke, I asked the group the same question. Almost every person in the room stood up. They all felt as though they knew Michael: by sharing his story, he made a difference and made the fight against colorectal cancer personal for the entire Exact Sciences team. Now, through his book, you too will have the opportunity to be inspired and empowered by his story and his moving words.

Backward

C. Zane Hagy
Ringleader
z11 communications
Oak Ridge, Tennessee

Writing a foreword to a book shouldn't be a daunting task. It's an honor, so I should just jump right in.

The problem is that I've read the book. It's better than I expected when I agreed to do this. It's heartwarming, inspiring, motivational and awe-inspiring. It's all the things that Michael Holtz is made of.

To truly introduce this book and Michael Holtz, I'd need more words than he used to tell his own story. So rather than try to do the impossible, and to do justice to this task, I opt to take another route and keep it simple.

We're all going to be faced with something in our lives that we think we cannot overcome. Before that time comes, I urge you to make time to read this book. Michael's incredible spirit to not just be alive but to truly live, regardless of the circumstances, comes through in the words on these pages.

He does the impossible and finds a way to infuse that spirit into the reader.

When I first met Michael, I wasn't that impressed. He always responded just a few seconds later than I thought he should. One day I realized why. He was listening more deeply and more closely than anyone else I'd ever met. When he responded, it was with thoughtfulness and meaning. In this book, Michael has taken his thoughtfulness and reason and turned it inward to share an amazing experience through cancer and beyond.

Read this now, before you need it. Keep it, and read it again when you do. Share it with someone else who is facing a challenge. Whatever you're facing, most likely it's not harder than cancer.

Acknowledgments

I'm one of those guys who has been thinking about writing a book for as long as I can remember. I even started writing a few times only to lose interest. Losing interest in your own life is a pretty sad state to be in when you think about it. My cancer experience was something different, though. While it borders on cliche to say cancer changed my life, it's also the truth. This book is the roadmap of those changes.

I am grateful to my medical team, who took such great care of me: Michael West, M.D., my primary care doctor at Summit Medical Group Norwood Clinic; Sarkis Chobanian, M.D., my gastoenterologist at Gastrointestinal Associates; Micheline Liebman, M.D., my oncologist at Thompson Cancer Survival Center; Joe Myer, M.D., my radiation oncologist; and Gregory Midis, M.D. my amazing and gifted surgeon at the Premier Surgical Associates Center for Advanced Medicine. I'm also thankful to all the nurses, nurse practitioners, radiation technologists, nutritionists and clerks who saw to it I was well cared for at every step during treatment.

Thanks also to my alternative medicine practitioners: Lynn Anderson, RN, for healing touch therapy, and Joel Packard, acupuncturist extraordinaire.

The Cancer Support Community of East Tennessee is a place where cancer patients, survivors and caregivers can find support among people who are headed down the same road. I'm grateful to Debra Sullivan, PhD, program director; Kathleen Williams, LCSW, program associate; and Beth Hamil, executive director. Thanks to my support group buddies Marie, Chuck, Juanita, Elizabeth, Andrew, Joe, Bonnie, Beth, Barbara and Charlotte, and everyone who was part of that journey. I met my dear friends Belinda and Kim in the CSCET art class, a chance meeting that really wasn't chance.

My former colleagues at the American Cancer Society and the American Cancer Society Cancer Action Network showed me the most incredible support. I'm especially grateful to my team in the Knoxville office: Jenny Stripling, Megan Brown, Amy Fields, Karen Gray, Sally Herron, Hope Mitchell, Stacy Hall, Sarah Hooks, Scotty Evans, Kayla Shelby, Wendi Klevan, Lauren Wey and Melody Harper; the entire ACS MidSouth Division team; and to Denise Billings, Robert Morris, Debra Wilson, Ginny Campbell, Kimberly Hughes, Anita Bales, Andrew Muhl, James Sharp, Eric Evans, Jason Brady, Lynn Williams, Nancy Hauskins-Dubois, Carter Steger, Erin O'Neill, Molly Daniels, Nicole Bender, Korinne Moore, Dustin Perchal, Kristin Nabers, Kelly Headrick, Steve Weiss, Katie Riley, Jeff Martin, Ann Goure, Hillary Clark, Sara Mannetter, Jen Hunt, and the rest of the ACS CAN staff in Washington, D.C., and around the country.

Thanks to everyone who brought us meals or sent cards and notes of support during treatment and surgery, especially Tina Price, Cheryl Ball, Charlie Tombras, Dooley Tombras and Linda Edwards. Thanks to our friends Duane and Kathy Ledford, Keith Parks, Angie Parks, Erin Parks, Sherry Morris, and John and Traci Frame, who brought laughter and love to our lives often during the journey.

My gym, Adaptive Fitness Warehouse, was an incredibly supportive place for a guy working to get his body back after treatment. Thanks to Adam Brown, Scarlet Strange, Lori Tucker, Christie Elliott, Lynn and Sandra Grubb, Grace and Brandon Reed, Billy Sapp, Sherineta Morrison, Jeff Bronson, Erin Donovan, Sharon Rivers, Tami Galik, Meghan Lovelace and Tiffany Harmening, all of whom were part of my fitness journey either in the box or on the field at boot camp.

I was humbled to be asked to use my marathon running and walking experience as a coach for the Leukemia and Lymphoma Society's Team In Training program walk team. Thanks to Anthony Palmer for asking me to coach, and to Patrick Gildea, Laurella Rochat, Michelle Hall, Julie Higgins Keller, Julie Maxwell Smith, Simone Guitard, Jim Hall and Richie Farr for their support and for their encouragement when I switched from coach to athlete.

Our church family at St. John's Lutheran Church has embraced us with grace and love. We're grateful to Rev. Steve and Jeanne Misenheimer, Rev. John Tirro and Misty

Anderson, and Rev. Amy Figg. Thanks also to Adam Schultz, Clark Hinkle, Brent Collins, John Rice, Marcia Powers, Ashton and Jennifer Roberts, John and Mary Cole, John and Sharon Stancher, Jim and Nancy Friedrich, Ron and Mary Rimer, Ruth Crowley, Rita Schwartz and so many others.

Bonnie Hufford, who is something of a second mother to both of us and an all-too-experienced cancer survivor, acted as our guide especially in the early days of our journey. It's horrible to be well-versed at first-hand cancer experiences, but we're grateful for Bonnie's knowledge.

We could not have gotten through this without our families. Thanks to Gloria Holtz; Brian, Jennifer, Christopher and Brandon Holtz; Tim, Terri, Miranda and Zachary Holtz; Rachael, Joe, Cloey and Ella Briere; Reece and Ruth Jamerson; Mark, Melinda, Mallie and Macy Jamerson; Cheri Jamerson; and Russell, Holly and Leah Jamerson.

Although they have been mentioned elsewhere, Sarah holds a special place in her heart for the friends and family who sat with her at the hospital while I was in surgery.

She will never forget Tina Price, Sherry Morris, Bonnie Hufford, Reece and Ruth Jamerson, Gloria Holtz, Rachael Holtz and Miranda Holtz for being with her that day. I'm grateful you were there for Sarah on a day more challenging than we anticipated.

I asked a small group of friends who happen to be fellow cancer survivors to read parts or all of the manuscript and give their honest feedback. What I got back were lots of glowing words from some wonderful people. Thanks to Jason Dean, Mary Cate and Kim Hansard for taking the time.

Thanks to Kevin Conroy, CEO at Exact Sciences, for agreeing to write the foreword when I asked. Exact Sciences is going to change the world, mark my word.

I'm grateful to Nan Harless for her editing skills, and for refining the finished product.

I can't thank Zane Hagy, my friend and brother from another mother, enough for his love, support and generosity of time during the writing process. As I wrote, he read, gave feedback and in many ways helped bring this book to life. There truly would be no book without him.

Last and certainly not least, there wouldn't be much of a story to tell were it not for the lovely Sarah, the best care-giver, partner and wife a guy could ever ask for. We've been through hell and back a couple of times, and her love, care and near superhuman emotional strength made survival possible for both of us. The mindsets I write about are not just mine. We share them. It's how we survived, together.

Introduction

I am a survivor.

Truth is, I seriously dislike that word. While it accurately describes coming out alive after a cancer experience, it is wholly inadequate. "Survivor" does not capture what it means to hear the words "you have cancer," or what it's like to have your rear end radiated to the point of blistering, or your body altered by surgery, or the physiological impact of steroids and poisonous chemicals administered week after week and month after month. "Survivor" also misses the psychological impact of the fear of death that arrives immediately upon diagnosis and the stress of recalibrating your entire life around treatment of the disease. For many of us, we come through the cancer experience with more than a touch of post-traumatic stress disorder.

We use the word "survivor" in the cancer community because it's quick shorthand to count the number of people who have lived past their diagnosis and treatment. In truth, that's all the word "survivor" is good for.

During my cancer experience, the members of my patient support group and I tried to come up with an alternate word. "Warrior" comes close, if you believe cancer is a battle and patients are fighting it. If you don't subscribe to the warlike imagery often used in describing cancer experiences, "warrior" definitely falls short.

In my life after cancer, I've come to prefer the term "thriver."

My life after cancer is thriving. I've had adventures I never anticipated: I participated in a tandem obstacle course race. I jumped into a startlingly cold river to celebrate the New Year. I became a gym owner. I preached in church. I went to the beach with my wife for the best vacation ever. I became a motivational speaker. And now I've written this book.

In short, life is amazing.

While it has become fashionable to say "cancer was a gift" or "cancer is the best thing that ever happened to me," I don't hold to that. If cancer was a gift, I'd return it to wherever in hell it came from. Rather, I believe having cancer enabled good things to happen. I value gratitude and love more than I ever have. I appreciate all of the amazing people in my life and do my best to not take for granted their presence in my life. I understand that caregivers are intensely undervalued.

I learned a lot during my cancer experience, which is why I wrote this book. I also wrote this book because when I went in search of books about colorectal cancer experiences, there were very few on the market. There are a lot of breast-cancer-specific books, however -- no offense to my sister survivors. Which brings me to another reason I wrote this book: very few books about personal cancer experiences are written by men. I felt the need to add my voice for that reason alone. Finally, the few books that do exist about colorectal cancer tend to be blow-by-blow tales of each author's cancer experience. That's not the story I wanted to tell.

Rather, I wanted to tell my story from the perspective of the mental attitudes it takes to survive and thrive after cancer. This is not a how-to book, though. I cannot give you the "three strategies you need to maintain a positive attitude during your illness." Honestly, much of what I write about comes to me naturally. Some I learned along the way, from great authors and from friends whose lives reflect the mindsets about which I write. Some of the mindsets, like being grateful in the face of difficulty and letting go of unnecessary emotions and obstacles, still take practice. In this book, I frame the mindsets around my story and how each of them worked for me.

While I cannot give you the "formula" for surviving and thriving, most chapters end with a Mindset Exercise, a simple exercise designed to help you think about how you can use each mindset in your own experience.

The title of this book comes directly from my response to some of the challenging but wonderful things I've done in the months and years since I finished treatment. Speak onstage about my cancer experience to a roomful of strangers? It's challenging, but it's not harder than cancer. Train to run a marathon with the intent of crossing the finish line more than an hour faster than ever before? Hard, but it's not harder than cancer. I've come to realize that even with a permanent colostomy, I can do just about anything I put my mind to doing. I have a robust bucket list, which you will read about in Chapter 10, and some of the items on it may feel in direct defiance of the fact that my body works differently than most people's bodies. It's difficult for some people to wrap their minds around the fact that I'm not sitting on the couch because of what I've been through. I'm just not that guy.

So, this is my story. It's a story of thriving through Stage-3b rectal cancer and some of the other ugliness of life, like childhood sexual abuse, a difficult paternal relationship and Rocky Mountain spotted fever. The details are not always pretty, but thanks be to God and the love and support of my friends and family, the end result is incredible.

Prologue: The Long Road

"God, my calves!" I said to myself as I made the turn onto Lakeshore Drive, which caresses the southern end of Lake Pontchartrain in New Orleans. "If I ever do this again, I have to wear compression socks."

I was walking, something I had not intended to be doing near mile 17 of the Rock 'n' Roll New Orleans Marathon. I had trained to "wog," a combination of walking and jogging, at intervals of three minutes of jogging to one minute of walking, with the intent of running some part of the entire race.

Four months of training back in Knoxville had prepared me, mentally and physically, for this day. I'd put in the time and done the mileage to be ready for this, my fifth marathon. To top it off, I was running for charity. I was part of the American Cancer Society's now mostly defunct DetermiNation program. On the back of my singlet, I had written the names of friends and family members who were fighting cancer or had died from the disease. It was a long list, and the memories of all the faces connected to the names propelled me to the finish line.

I had not fought cancer. I didn't know a thing about chemotherapy or radiation therapy, except what I had read in books or on our company website. It sounded horrible. In my mind, if cancer patients could endure the rigors of cancer treatment, I could wog a marathon to raise a little bit of money.

It was hot, though, for a marathon, with temperatures in the upper 70s, and the heat was taking its toll. Salt had leached though my pores as I dripped with sweat. I could feel granules on my face, making it feel like sandpaper. Sweat mingled with the salt on my eyelids, causing me to tear up. Leaching salt put my electrolytes off balance, as evidenced by my cramping calf muscles.

I knew from experience that the cramps could have been worse. A year earlier I wogged the Country Music Marathon in Nashville. Race-day temperatures soared to the upper 80s very quickly. I couldn't drink water fast enough to stay hydrated. My calf muscles cramped so severely during the last six miles that I had to stop every 100 feet or so to stretch in an effort to get them to calm down. My coach, an amazing Ironman athlete named Shahin Hadian, astride his bicycle and searching for me, handed me a small plastic bag of salt tablets.

"Take two of these every mile," he said, before riding off to find another member of our training team.

I didn't know until days later that while Shahin was making sure I and the rest of our team finished the race, his dad was dying of leukemia in Toronto. Michael Hadian may well have breathed his last while his son was giving me a packet of salt tablets.

That thought, and the opportunity to train with Shahin and the rest of the friends I'd made at Fleet Feet Knoxville, gave me reason to sign up for another stint as a DetermiNation athlete. Michael Hadian's name was among those on the back of my shirt in 2012, along with the following:

- Nancy, a dear friend who was diagnosed with ductal breast cancer before Christmas 2011. She is an amazing stage actress who happens also to be a survivor.

- John, a friend and colleague who was diagnosed with recurrent cancer in the summer of 2011. The disease would take him before the end of 2012.

- Jeffrey, a 20-year survivor of brain cancer who was experiencing a recurrence.

- Emily, the mother of one of my colleagues and friends, who would eventually succumb to Stage-4 lung cancer.

- Bonnie, a friend I've known since I moved to Knoxville in 1992. She battled leukemia for much of her life and added multiple myeloma to the mix, just for the hell of it.

- Marilyn, one of the strongest women I have ever known and a fierce cancer advocate. Cancer took her away in December 2011.

- Bob, my uncle and the first person I ever knew to be diagnosed with cancer. He died of pancreatic cancer when I was 21.

Those names and faces kept me focused on making it to the finish. The cramps in my calf muscles never got as bad as in Nashville, likely because I swallowed as much salt and electrolyte-replacement drink as I could.

There was something else: I'd had to stop to use a port-o-let at mile 10. My intestines had been gurgling warning signs for about two miles. I had tried to put the urge to use the bathroom out of my mind -- after all I'd never, ever stopped to do more than pee during a race. But the urge was unrelenting: I had to go.

That pit stop put me completely off my rhythm. As I reached mile 12.5 and saw the turn toward the half-marathon finish line to the right, I wondered if I shouldn't just chuck the second half and follow the crowd. As with most marathons, the vast majority of participants at Rock 'n' Roll New Orleans were running the half. Half the distance, half the training, half the time on the course.

As I looked right, I saw all the great spectator support and heard the PA announcer reading off names as athletes crossed the finish line. As I looked left, I saw not one person in front of me, not one person on the sidelines, just a long line of orange cones marking the way ahead.

My head and my heart argued.

"You could cross the finish line in less than 15 minutes," my head said, "and be eating beignets at Cafe du Monde with the lovely Sarah within an hour."

"This is not what you signed up for," my heart shot back. "Remember why you're doing this."

I arrived at the turn. It was decision time. Of course, I chose the long, lonely second half. It was what I'd trained for, what I'd flown to New Orleans to do, why I had a list of names emblazoned on the back of my shirt.

And I was healthy. The healthiest I'd ever been, in fact. I had spent the previous two years working hard to lose weight by exercising and watching what I ate. As a result, I'd lost 100 pounds. My weight loss was so significant, I was wearing clothing sizes I hadn't fit into since sophomore year of high school.

I pressed on, miles 17 through 22, along Lakeshore Drive. I heard a cowbell as I made the turn from Lakeshore onto Marconi Drive.

"More cowbell!" I shouted, as I kept trucking along. There was more cowbell.

Marconi Drive runs along the edge of City Park, where the finish line was located. I'd already gone up the three miles of Marconi toward Lakeshore; now it was time to finish this.

Knowing the end of the race was near, I felt my pace pick up. I heard "Walking on Sunshine," by Katrina and the Waves, in my head. At least I think it was in my head, as I had trained myself to run without a gadget pumping tunes into my ears.

Before long I was winding my way through the last 1.2 miles of the course in City Park. Sad thing was, because I was one of the last finishers, not much of the finish line remained. The chutes were still standing, but volunteers and event staff were already pulling down signage and dismantling the refreshment stations. The finish-line party in the park was already over. I managed to grab a couple bananas, a bagel and a bottle of water. Someone held out a finisher medal. I grabbed it. In the chaos, Sarah and I found each other.

"I'm never doing this again," I said to her, a catch in my voice, somewhere between the finish line and our walk toward the DetermiNation tent. "It's just too hard. It's too much work, and I'm never going to be fast."

My finish time was 6:21:11. Slow, yes, but 15 minutes or so faster than my time at the Country Music Marathon the year before. It was a personal record. Maybe, I thought to myself, I could finish my next race in under six hours. Never say never.

Three weeks later, we would be on the path of an entirely different marathon.

Chapter 1 - The Treatment Marathon

"You have cancer."

Three words that changed my life in an instant. Words that Dr. Sarkis Chobanian, my gastroenterologist, was shocked he was telling me just five days after my 43rd birthday.

He expected to tell me I had celiac disease or maybe colitis. I was hoping for celiac disease myself. "Hoping" for celiac disease may sound odd, but in retrospect, a lifetime of eating gluten-free food would have been the far better choice.

I'd even read about the increasing prevalence of celiac in a book called *Wheat Belly*, by William Davis, MD, a cardiologist. Davis postulates that celiac disease, the insulin resistance that causes weight gain and other ailments, can be traced to all of the genetic modifications that make wheat hardier and more plentiful. The wheat we eat today has a higher glycemic index that sugar, he says.

After reading the book, and because I had been experiencing several months of funky digestive symptoms that lined up with many of the symptoms Davis listed in his book, I decided to give up any foods that contained wheat or gluten on a trial basis.

It wasn't easy. Every food label had to be carefully examined. Wheat flour show up in a lot of unexpected places, like candy and soup. Still, for two weeks I avoided consuming wheat in any form. The weird symptoms I had been experiencing -- feeling the urge to move my bowels with nothing happening on the one hand, or barely making it to the toilet on the other -- seemed to get better. My bathroom experiences seemed to be getting back to "normal."

Then came Valentine's Day. I took Sarah out for a great dinner at a new restaurant. I knew even before we sat down to eat that I was going to have wheat-based foods, like bread and a cupcake. I regretted that decision later. My stomach roiled. The symptoms that had eased up returned with a vengeance. Of course I saw this as proof that I had celiac disease.

A week or so later, I noticed the blood. Not a lot, but there it was one day, floating on top of the water in the toilet.

I knew from my work at the American Cancer Society that blood in the toilet and in my stool was not a good sign. I made an appointment with my primary care physician, Dr. Michael West, who said his knee-jerk reaction was to refer me for a colonoscopy. While theoretically I was too young, the blood was definitely a concern.

Which is how, ultimately, I ended up reading a preliminary report about the nine-centimeter undifferentiated adenocarcinoma that had grown in my rectum. On the screen capture Dr. Chobanian gave us, the tumor looked like a big ugly tarry black spot.

"You didn't do anything to cause it, and you couldn't have done anything to prevent it," Dr. Chobanian said. "It's the luck of the genetic draw."

I was lucky to have Dr. Chobanian on my medical team. He is the best of the best when it comes to gastroenterologists in Knoxville. He was President Ronald Reagan's gastroenterologist. Whatever he said, we were going to believe.

He went on to tell us that he would see me again in a year for a follow-up colonoscopy, after a difficult few months of battling the cancer. In the meantime, I would undergo an endoscopic ultrasound and a full-body PET scan and meet with a surgeon. He recommended a guy named Gregory Midis, who had a great reputation in treating cases like mine.

That day, the day I was diagnosed, was surreal, like something out of a David Lynch movie. We went from my gastroenterologist's office to lunch, then to visit our close friends Duane and Kathy, whose young son Aaron died that very morning of a seeming mystery illness that turned out to be cancer.

In all the hubbub to get me off the examination table and into the doctor's office so Dr. Chobanian could share my diagnosis in private, I never got to the farting part. For those who have never had a colonoscopy, the medical team blows air up your ass to help the colonoscope find its way. After the procedure, the expectation is that you blow the air back out. I didn't get the chance, and I could feel the air trapped in my gut while we were sitting with Duane and Kathy, doing everything we could to console them in their time of profound grief. These were some of our closest friends, and Sarah and I decided we could not, not on this day anyway, share my diagnosis with them. It would have to wait.

What couldn't wait, though, was the air trapped in my gut. I needed to go home. I was in pain as the trapped air moved around. Things were going to get indelicate and wildly inappropriate if I didn't get out of there.

Sarah took me home and then returned to be with our friends. Adding to the surreal, Sarah accompanied Duane and Kathy to the funeral home so they could make final arrangements. Meanwhile, I found the relief I needed and worked my way through the list of people we felt should know about my diagnosis.

To add to the Lynchian aspect of that first day after diagnosis, sleep didn't come easily – that night or for several after, actually. It wasn't worry about cancer or dying that kept me awake. Rather, I felt an odd throbbing in my backside, as if simply recognizing that a tumor was there had brought the thing to life. The new, alive thing was making its presence known. I know it was totally psychosomatic, but that aggressive tumor felt like it was growing as I thought about it.

When I reported this on a subsequent visit with my oncologist, she prescribed Ambien to help me get through the night. Prescribing sleep aids for cancer patients is not uncommon. I wonder, though, how many of us actually believe we can feel our tumors throbbing inside us.

In our initial meeting with my surgeon, we found Dr. Midis to be gregarious, caring, optimistic and, quite frankly, wonderful. He was also a distance runner, which was an unlikely subject to discuss while I was lying on the table undergoing a flexible sigmoidoscopy.

"Slow, deep breaths," he said, as the sigmoidoscope was threaded up my ass like a pipe snake. "So, what was your time in the half-marathon?"

I don't remember that I answered, but I do remember squirming on the table, as this particular rear-entry examination wasn't preceded by a sleep-inducing dose of propofol. It would not be the first injustice done to my hindquarters.

Still, the meeting with Dr. Midis was a blessing. He told us my PET scan was clear, meaning the cancer had not spread and was localized to the rectum. He wanted me to have an MRI before surgery so he could make sure my pelvis was absolutely clear, but there was no reason to believe the cancer had spread beyond the primary site.

Dr. Midis also laid out the schedule and the treatment plan for the months ahead. I had Stage-3b cancer, which meant the tumor was growing rather aggressively and there was some lymph node involvement. He sat down with us and drew out the treatment plan. Stage-3 cancer had a standard treatment plan, delivered in three parts:

- Radiation therapy and oral chemotherapy: 28 sessions of radiation concurrent with 55 days taking a drug called Xyloda.

- Surgery: Two months after the end of radiation, Dr. Midis would remove what remained of the tumor. The two-month waiting period was required because the tissue around the tumor site was very fragile and needed time to heal.

- Chemotherapy: Twelve rounds of infused chemotherapy delivered every other week over six months. In addition to spending a huge chunk of every other Wednesday at Thompson Cancer Survival Center getting infused with a drug cocktail called FOLFOX, I would take a pump home for two days to finish the process.

Over the next couple of weeks I met my oncologist, Dr. Micheline Liebman, and radiation oncologist, Dr. Joe Meyer. We scheduled treatment dates and talked through the processes for each.

Dr. Liebman was relatively reassuring. Xyloda might cause numbness and tingling in my hands and feet, she said, or cause blistering in my mouth, but I was not going to lose my hair, and it was unlikely that I would experience much in the way of nausea and vomiting. Still, she prescribed anti-nausea medication, just in case.

Oral chemo was easy, at least when compared to everything else I endured during the 11 months between diagnosis and my last infused chemotherapy appointment. I simply had to swallow a bunch of pills a couple times a day and monitor myself for side effects. Except for a weird ringing in my head that started almost from the moment I took the first couple of Xyloda, I didn't experience anything else in the way of side effects.

Dr. Meyer was also reassuring but wanted me to have more realistic expectations. I could expect some serious side effects. Radiation therapy is cumulative: I was likely to experience fatigue, and I could expect to get blisters in my "gluteal crease," as Dr. Meyer called my crack.

Two things needed to happen before I started radiation therapy. First, I had to get a mold made of my legs and hips, lying ass-up. I would get into this mold whenever I climbed onto the linear accelerator's table. The mold would hold my body in proper position every time and keep me from moving. Then I had to get my ass "tattooed": Xs in three places, one on each cheek and one centered over the top of my crack -- points at which the techs would aim the radiation.

Once I started radiation therapy, I was amazed at how quickly each session ended. For most of the 28 sessions, I was in and out in under 15 minutes, including check-in, dropping trou and getting dressed again. Only the sessions that also included a visit with Dr. Meyer lasted longer. As promised, blisters developed in my crack during the last week of radiation therapy, so much so that my anus swelled open. There was leakage.

"Is this normal?" I asked the nurse.

"Yes," she said, "I'm afraid it is. You might consider adding padding or wearing adult diapers until things go back to normal."

So there I was, walking into the drugstore to procure adult diapers. This was right around the time Depend was marketing a new line of products that were "closer to real underwear." Uh, yeah, if you wear underwear made of paper lined with plastic. They were gray, like some crazy cross between something that might have been the norm in 1960s Soviet Russia and something issued by Big Brother in George Orwell's *1984*. Still, I wasn't wearing Depends because they were fashionable but because they would absorb whatever leaked out of my backside.

About the wad of padding that ran from front to back: talk about uncomfortable. I felt like I was walking around with a full diaper all the time. I now have serious empathy for women who use maxi pads during their "special" time of the month. I'm thankful I had to don the adult diapers only for a couple of weeks until the leakage stopped.

If I knew then what I know now, though, I would have appreciated the last two months of my fully functioning but tumor-ridden rectum. Two months was the length of time between my last radiation therapy session and surgery to remove the tumor.

Anytime we met with Dr. Midis, from our initial meeting post-diagnosis to the last meeting before we saw him in the hospital, he talked about going in, cutting the cancer out, and then reconnecting the cut ends of my rectum. I would require a temporary colostomy, but Dr. Midis was going to put me back together.

It wasn't until the morning of surgery that Dr. Midis raised the possibility of a permanent colostomy. He drew two circles on my abdomen, one on each side of my belly button. The circles were over the rectus abdominis muscles, through which he would punch a hole and thread the cut end of my colon. My poo would empty into a bag adhered to my body. As he drew the circles, he explained what they meant.

"If I use the right side, the colostomy is temporary," he said. "If it's the left, it's permanent. I have to be prepared for both, but we're going to put you back together again."

Our pastor, dear, sweet Amy Figg, met us at the hospital very early that Friday morning. We talked, laughed and prayed before I was wheeled away to surgery. The last thing I remember was being very cold and naked in the surgery suite after sliding off the wide and comfortable gurney and onto a very narrow and uncomfortable surgical table.

I awoke feeling very hot and sweaty, with fans blowing air over my body as recovery nurses worked to lower my temperature. I heard someone, one of the nurses, call my name as I slowly became aware of my surroundings. Nurses moved about. I was so hot. I was so thirsty. And my back hurt. And what were the weird contraptions on my legs, adding and then removing pressure like some jacked-up massage device?

"I made it through the surgery," I thought to myself, then nodded out again.

When I awoke the next time, I was in my hospital room. Sarah, my mom and others were in the room. The nurse was working to make me comfortable. I had been on my back for hours, she said, and it probably hurt.

"I'll put some extra pillows under you, starting with the left side, where all the action was," she said.

The left side?

Not the left side.

"Shit," I thought to myself, "it's permanent." Followed quickly by: "It could be worse. I'm still here."

Dr. Midis came in a few minutes after I was settled into my room. His face and countenance were not that of the man I saw earlier that day. He was downcast and dispirited. He explained that the tumor was larger than he originally thought, and scarring from radiation therapy left little usable tissue with which to work. The entire rectum had to be removed.

He added that the hospital's ostomy nurses would be in touch soon to help me understand how to attach and change the necessary pouching system that would keep me alive. In the meantime, a pouch had been attached while I was in surgery. A nurse came in at regular intervals to measure what I expelled to the pouch, as well as into a urinary catheter bag and a drain tube snaked into my pelvis. There were odd tubes everywhere. But I was alive.

As promised, the ostomy nurses, Ann and Jordana, visited once a day for three days to teach me and Sarah how to change my appliance. First, I learned how to cut a hole in the "wafer," the piece that sticks to my abdomen by way of an adhesive bandage. My stoma, the name given to the end of my colon now sticking through my abdomen, has to fit through the hole. Second, I learned to put a bead of pectin paste around the cut edges as an added level of security against leakage. Finally, I had to learn to snap on a new pouch, which attaches not unlike Tupperware to a plastic ring on the wafer.

On day one, the nurses walked through the entire process while we observed. On the second day, I did the work with assistance from Ann and Jordana. By the last day, I was able to attach the appliance by myself while the nurses watched. I can honestly say I've never had so many eyes on my butthole (well, my new one) at any one time in my life.

In the hospital, I used drainable pouches. A clip on the lower end of the pouch is undone, allowing waste to flow out and into the toilet. Most ostomates, the name given to people with ostomies, can sit on the toilet, unclip their bag and drain it into the toilet below. However, my thighs are too broad to make this work. And kneeling before the throne to drain a pouch isn't practical in any workplace or travel situation. As a result I use disposable bags that snap off and can be tossed in the trash in opaque bags designed for the very purpose. It's very convenient.

Except for the occasional humiliating and heart-stopping pouch blowout, there are worse things than shitting into a bag. My morning routine is shorter, and I can do almost anything I did before I had the colostomy. In fact, I've been more active with the colostomy than I was before cancer. I work out, take part in obstacle course races and swim. Ann and Jordana promised life wouldn't have to stop just because of the plastic bag attached to my abdomen. I've made sure they're right. I do miss farting, though.

Six weeks after surgery, in late September, I started chemotherapy, every other Wednesday for six months. Chemo was relatively uneventful. I read a lot of books while sitting in the infusion room waiting for the chemo to enter my bloodstream, and I took a pump home for two days to finish the process.

While a number of side effects were possible, including sensitivity to cold, nausea, vomiting, mouth blisters and neuropathy, only the cold sensitivity really presented itself. For the first week after every chemo session, I could not put my hand in the refrigerator or freezer without what felt like an electric shock coursing through my nerves. Then, as the weather got colder -- the perils of undergoing chemo during the winter months -- I had to be careful to cover my mouth when I went outdoors. In severe cases, the cold sensitivity can make some patients feel like they can't breathe. Anytime I was out in the cold, I was either wrapped in a scarf or wore a gator over my head. Honestly, grabbing a Diet Dr. Pepper out of the refrigerator was more difficult than walking the dog, as far as cold sensitivity was concerned.

Neuropathy, the sensation of numbness in my hands and feet, arrived a month after I finished chemo. Neuropathy is a common chemotherapy complaint, but it doesn't often present after treatment. My situation stymied my oncologist because she or the nurse practitioner I saw on my appointments had been careful to ask if I was feeling any numbness and tingling. If ever the answer had been yes, they would have reduced one of the drugs in my FOLFOX cocktail. Alas, my neuropathy arrived after.

What sucked about neuropathy for me was that I couldn't feel the ground beneath my feet. On more than one occasion, I fell down. In one memorable episode, I was walking the dog when I stepped wrong. I could feel myself falling but couldn't stop it from happening. I slid across the pavement, scraping the palms of my hands and both knees. Marley, the dog, was smart enough to get out of the way of the large man falling toward her.

Ultimately, the neuropathy problem was solved by a combination of acupuncture and medication. It took nearly a year, but the feeling in my hands and feet has returned to near normal, aside from lingering cold in my feet that occurs when the temperature drops.

As for the rest of me, I've also returned to near normal, whatever that is, since chemotherapy ended, enabling me to look forward to what I hope is a long life filled with hope, gratitude and happiness.

Michael Holtz

Chapter 2: Love Your Caregiver

"I really, really don't like the word 'caregiver.' It's so ... inadequate to capture the depth and breadth of the situation. We need to call it something else." -- Sarah Holtz

I agree with the lovely Sarah: "Caregiver" is a wholly inadequate term for the person or persons who share the experience with the cancer patient. Cancer patients have one job: to get well. Caregivers, on the other hand, take care of all the details involved in the care of the patient.

Sarah made sure I got to all my medical appointments, and she prepared for them so she could ask questions of the medical team. She insured medications were taken as prescribed. She made sure I ate, stayed hydrated, rested, bathed and moved, even if it was a short walk to the mailbox. She asked whether I experienced neuropathy between chemo sessions. She made sure I wasn't spiraling into depression by asking how I felt emotionally and whether I felt suicidal.

She also fielded most of the outbound communication to family and friends when I was in the hospital for surgery. Sarah had a list of people she or I wanted to make sure got called with an update about surgery. She made all those calls.

Except for a few hours on the second and third days after my surgery, Sarah never left my side in the hospital. She spent uncomfortable nights on a pullout bed. Those few hours she was away she used to take a nap and get a shower. When she was away, she made arrangements to have someone in the room with me at all times.

Being a caregiver means wearing a lot of different hats.

The thing is, caregivers often get overlooked during the cancer experience. Everyone wants to know how the patient is doing, but few people ask the caregiver how he or she is doing. It's unfortunate. Sarah was doing all the day-to-day work.

Take it from me: It's important to love your caregiver. You can tell him or her that you do, but you should also be a good patient. Cancer is hard, and it would be so easy to get cranky and hateful because of the multiple traumas you are experiencing physically, psychologically or financially. If you need a place to vent, find a support group, a therapist or a trusted friend. Whatever you do, do not take out your frustrations on your caregiver. Just as you didn't ask to be diagnosed with a serious illness, your caregiver didn't ask to be given the burden he or she now bears. Love, honor and respect his or her role in the process. Treat your caregivers well. I promise you, they're making the best they can of a bad situation.

In addition to all of the organization and logistics, Sarah also carried the bulk of the fear for us. Most pointedly, she was the one who worried about whether I was going to die. I learned that the hard way after an appointment with my radiation oncologist.

We had been getting the full-court press to get a second opinion about my treatment plan from a friend, a longtime cancer survivor who had experienced several recurrences during her life. She urged us both to go to the

Vanderbilt-Ingram Cancer Center at Vanderbilt University Medical Center in Nashville. She even did research for us and found the exact surgeon we should see. The only thing was, I was perfectly comfortable with Dr. Midis, whose reputation was solid.

Still, Sarah asked my radiation oncologist whether we should get a second opinion from the surgeon in Nashville. He said two things that, in my mind, completely shut down the need to get a second opinion.

"If I were in your shoes, I would have Dr. Midis do my surgery," and "You can get a second opinion, but keep in mind that a resident may actually do your surgery under his supervision."

Nope. Not going to happen. I know residents need to gain experience in the surgical suite, but I wasn't willing to be an experiment. I held my tongue until we got in the car. Fact is, I was kind of a jerk about the whole issue.

"We're done talking about getting a second opinion," I said.

"So, I don't get consideration here?" she responded.

"I'm not going to risk being cut open by a resident. I'm done talking about it."

"Okay."

Only it wasn't, because then the tears started.

"What's wrong?" I asked, clearly irritated.

She let me know she was frustrated that I completely shut down the discussion about a second opinion. We were in unknown territory. She's made a career being a project manager, and this was one project she didn't know how to manage. There were no clear right or wrong steps to take to get to the best possible end. And she was afraid -- most of all of losing me -- and wasn't it worth our time to investigate getting the best possible care we could?

"I'm seeing the best colon surgeon with the best reputation in town," I said. "I don't feel the need to talk to anyone else about this, and waiting to get a second opinion could mean a delay in getting treatment. I don't want to delay. I want to get this started."

Somehow we both reached agreement, or at least stasis, to stay on the path outlined by Dr. Midis.

I was relieved. If Sarah was scared, she never showed it again. Even on the day of my surgery, she was as strong as I've ever seen her. She was amazing through my entire course of treatment. In fact, I know I wouldn't be alive today without her love and care.

It wasn't the first time, either.

Almost eight years earlier, in the fall of 2004, I was diagnosed with a mild case of Rocky Mountain spotted fever, a tick-borne illness somewhat common in the Great Smoky Mountains National Park.

I was in Nashville for a work meeting, the state Relay for Life Summit. It was a two-day event, the first night of which ended with a concert. I was feeling a little flu-like, not surprisingly as I had been burning the candle at both ends with a very busy job as regional communications specialist for four markets in the state. I decided to retire early and headed up to my hotel room.

During the night, a fever broke out. I shivered myself awake several times through the night. I got up when the alarm went off and dragged myself to the bathroom. I passed out while peeing, taking out the towel rack as I fell and landing in the small space between the toilet and the bathtub. It's a miracle I didn't split my head open on all the porcelain. I did, however, finish peeing on the way down, which made a lovely mess all over the floor.

Ultimately, I ended up being taken to Montgomery County Medical Center by ambulance.

My boss or a co-worker called Sarah to let her know I was headed to the hospital. She hates hospitals. In fact, she hates anything having to do with medicine whatsoever. It stems from childhood trauma and re-trauma from a series of medical problems. The crinkly white paper on examination tables combined with the antiseptic smell of medical facilities makes her absolutely nauseated.

She seriously panicked when I had to take her to the emergency room when we were dating. She had injured her back stepping off the back porch of the house where I lived. She couldn't move, and pain was shooting up her leg and her back. In the ER, Sarah screamed, "Don't let them keep me!" as the clerk put an identification bracelet on her wrist.

To her credit, Sarah is calm in a crisis. We both are. In the case of my Rocky Mountain spotted fever episode, she quickly wrapped up a visit with her friend Tina, who advised her to pack a bag "just in case," then headed to Nashville.

I spent four days in the hospital, where I was infused with hard-core antibiotics to fight the tick-borne bacteria. Weirdly, there was no evidence of a tick bite, but I let doctors know I had been hiking on Mt. Cammerer in the Smokies the previous weekend. Blood titers indicated I was positive for a very mild, but clearly effective, case of tick-borne illness.

Although it was uncomfortable, Sarah stayed on the pullout bed the entire time I was hospitalized. No freaking out about being in the hospital. She left for only a couple hours to buy clothes, as she'd inadvertently packed nothing but underwear.

She was equally calm after my cancer diagnosis. Aside from that moment in the car, I never saw her crack again. She was stoic and strong from the moment of diagnosis, through all phases of treatment, through surgery and my hospital stay. While we were learning to change my colostomy appliance, I pooped. Freaked me out. She was nonplussed.

As I said earlier, I am alive today because of her strength and care. I'm an incredibly lucky man.

And to think, we almost didn't happen.

Sarah and I met in August 1992, on the first day of graduate school in the College of Communications at the University of Tennessee. As Sarah tells the story, it was love at first sight -- for her. At some point during our first semester, I did a presentation on the rise of conservative media, and she was hooked. Embarrassingly, I hadn't been paying attention. In truth, I wasn't terribly interested in a relationship. I'd had a girlfriend in high school and college who was high maintenance and overly dramatic. Our relationship had ended badly -- a bit like *Fatal Attraction* without the boiled bunny. I wasn't ready to jump in the pool again, but Sarah was already in the water.

Not only did we go to school together, we also worked together. I was editor of what was then called the *West*

Knox/Farragut Press Enterprise, a newspaper that served the bedroom community of Farragut and the rest of the western end of Knox County. She was a reporter who was working on a series of stories about local houses of worship. I was still clueless.

Eventually I caught on, thanks to the help of a friend. I was flattered, somewhat interested and a whole lot afraid. Still, I decided there was no harm in our being friends.

Our first "date" was a horrifying outing with a group of our grad school friends. We went to the movies. Our every action was observed by a dozen other people. It was like being an ant under a microscope, and I could feel my ass starting to burn.

We spent a lot of time together, as friends. Dinner, movies, conversation, coffee. For my part, I would have let it continue that way, but a friend asked whether I liked Sarah romantically. I said I did, to which he replied that I needed to step up and ask her to be my girlfriend. So one day I bought flowers, dressed in a shirt and tie and made plans to take Sarah to Aubrey's, a favorite restaurant of ours.

Nervously, I knocked on Sarah's door. The truth was, I knew in my heart I loved her and wanted to spend as much time with her as possible. I wanted that time to start immediately. She saw the flowers and the tie and realized our relationship had changed.

Sarah told me later that I came to my senses in the nick of time. She had grown frustrated with the glacier-slow pace of our relationship progress and was going to tell me she didn't want to see me anymore. Then she saw me with those flowers.

Exactly a year later, I proposed to Sarah. It took some planning, and we had some serious conversation about engagement, but in the end we wanted to spend the rest of our lives together. So when the time came to pop the question, I put together an elaborate plan to do it just right.

Whenever we talked about getting married, Sarah said she wanted an engagement Jeep instead of an engagement ring. She was joking, I know, but that figured into my plan.

Because of my work at the newspaper, I had become good friends with Randy Burleson, the owner of Aubrey's, which was just one restaurant at the time. Today there are nine Aubrey's restaurants throughout our region, and he owns a host of other great establishments, but I digress.

Together, Randy and I hatched a plan that rolled out like this: Sarah and I arrived at the restaurant for lunch. A vase of roses was on our table. She was surprised, but I love to give her flowers, so they were not entirely unexpected. We ate our lunch. Before dessert, a remote-control car -- not quite a Jeep, but an adequate substitution -- rolled down the aisle bearing a ring box that contained my mother's wedding ring. The car stopped, I got down on one knee, removed the ring from the box and asked Sarah to be my wife.

She didn't answer the question, but then it was difficult to hear over the din of the entire newspaper staff and a somewhat crowded restaurant applauding what had just occurred. Diane, my photographer, was snapping photos of the moment, which Sarah only realized later. After lunch, we went to Anchor Park in Farragut, where, sitting on a swing, I reminded Sarah she had not answered the question. Frankly, at this point I was a little worried she was going to turn me down. After nearly ending our relationship once already, I wouldn't have blamed her.

"I didn't want to answer in the spotlight," she said, then paused. "Yes, I will marry you."

I was over the moon. We both were. I was going to marry the woman I loved.

We got married on April 20, 1996. Ours was a beautiful ceremony filled with music, poetry and important verses of Scripture. Sarah and I planned a beautiful ceremony -- I was no parachute groom, after all, and Sarah and her mom planned a great reception. Attendance was much lower than we expected because tornadoes and thunderstorms had blown through the region that day. Those storms were nothing like the one we would encounter 16 years later.

Sarah really was remarkable through the whole cancer thing, as strong as I have ever seen her. She also proved to be very adaptable. A lot of change happened during our cancer year: my body was altered, some longtime friends disappeared, and our love for each other deepened considerably. Amazing what a health crisis can do to steel a marriage.

In addition to facing cancer together, we expanded our family by adopting a dog. Okay, I played the cancer card. I'm not ashamed. I had cancer, dammit!

I had wanted a dog from the time we were married. We even had a dog for a short time after we moved into our house in 1998. His name was Rookie. He was a Welsh corgi who dug into the yard of one of Sarah's co-workers. Brian spread the word around the neighborhood, but no one claimed him. So we did. Rookie was beautiful -- and intact, which meant he pissed on just about everything in our house. When I walked him, I had to get him about a mile from the house before he would do his business, which wasn't always convenient. In addition, he needed a lot of attention, which neither Sarah nor I had the ability to give. Ultimately we decided he had to go. I found a family at work that had a fenced-in yard and a houseful of kids. They took

Rookie, and as far as we know, he lived a long and happy life.

Our experience with Rookie left Sarah hesitant to bring another dog into our home. During radiation therapy, though, I decided it was time to get a dog.

"I'm 43 years old, and I have cancer," I said. "I want a dog."

Sarah couldn't really argue with me, but she wanted to hold off until we found the perfect dog.

"You fall in love with every dog you see. We need to find one that fits us."

She was right. We visited a couple of pet adoption events in our community, and I would have opened our home to half the dogs we saw, whether or not they were too big, too rambunctious, too shy, whatever -- I would have taken them.

On the other hand, my calm, organized wife searched petfinder.com and found a dog she thought would be perfect. This dog was a golden retriever/basset hound mix who was being fostered by a volunteer for the Tennessee Valley

Golden Retriever Rescue. She was a year old, a smaller-sized dog with a great personality. The only drawback was that she had chewed a couple of her previous owner's throw rugs.

I emailed the group's director asking about their adoption process and how we might meet the dog we were interested in. It took two months of back-and-forth conversation, but we finally met "our dog" when the group had an adoption event at the pet-supply store near our house. The group required a home visit before they would release the dog, so we could come to the store, meet the dog, have our home visit, and if all went well, we'd be considered for adoption.

We arrived at the store, both of us excited but nervous. Sarah was reliving Rookie moments; I was looking forward to adopting a dog.

Then we saw her: Marley, the smartest dog in the world. She was perfect. Golden, bright-eyed, small enough to fit in our small house. I wanted to get closer.

I got down on the floor to be closer to her, which physically hurt my rear end because I had just finished my last round of radiation therapy the day before the adoption event. Marley immediately climbed into my lap and settled in.

We were hooked on each other.

"I'm doomed, aren't I?" Sarah asked.

"Yeah, I think you are," I said.

There was still the minor issue of the home visit, though. We drove the executive director the one-mile distance to our house. She came in, looked around, saw we weren't pet hoarders and approved us for adoption.

"You can take her home today if you would like," she said.

We went back to the pet store, handed over the adoption fee, bought a leash and went on our way with our new fur child.

We were hers and she was ours from the moment she hopped in the car with us. We stopped for lunch and sat on the patio with Marley. The restaurant was relatively busy, but Marley stayed by my side the entire time.

She's been with us for two years now, and Marley is a much-loved and much-spoiled member of our family.

I got the chance to be Sarah's caregiver in late May of 2013, when she experienced an acute gallbladder attack. If I had to guess, I would say she had been in pain for months, including months when I was in chemo, but because she was taking care of me, she was focusing away from her own pain.

I was supposed to travel to Washington, D.C., for work, my first meeting with colleagues from around the country since two months after my diagnosis. I was really looking forward to the trip, but I bowed out when I realized Sarah was in too much pain to get out of bed. She had refused to see a doctor, so she wasn't even on pain medication.

I took her to the emergency room. During an ultrasound, the tech confirmed what we already suspected: her gallbladder was loaded with stones and would have to come out. My love was going to have surgery.

Sarah did not freak out this time when she was admitted to the hospital. She says she was in so much pain that she would have done anything to make it go away, including getting cut in five different places to get her gallbladder out. We learned later that the gallbladder was necrotizing, and Sarah likely would have died if I had left her and headed to D.C.

I stayed with her in the hospital. All right, it was just one night, but I stayed. At home, I made sure she ate and took her pain meds and bathed. Comparatively speaking, I did very little for Sarah, and she did so much for me, but we'll both tell you we saved each other's life.

Because I was recovering from surgery and then started chemotherapy during the fall of 2012, we missed our annual vacation. We would have preferred to be anywhere other than our every-other-week visits to the infusion room. Cancer treatment certainly wasn't restful or relaxing.

I made it up to Sarah in 2013, when we spent a week at one of our favorite places on earth: the historic King and Prince Beach and Golf Resort on St. Simons Island,

Georgia. We had been there two or three times before, so we were familiar with the restaurants and tourist attractions in the area. We also knew we loved the hotel. That week of sitting on lounge chairs on the pool deck, which also overlooked the beach, and eating at restaurants like the Fourth of May Cafe was the perfect way to celebrate the end of treatment, the beginning of life after cancer and the fact that we were both still alive, given the medical experiences we'd had. We could, for the most part, put what we had been through out of our minds and focus on the sun, water and waves.

It was our best vacation ever. We knew that there would be follow-up medical appointments for years to come and that we would live forever with the omnipresent possibility of a cancer recurrence, but we made it through. We did it together. Our relationship and our marriage are stronger because of our cancer experience.

Mindset Exercise

Many people diagnosed with cancer or other serious illness have a spouse or significant other they can rely on to be their caregiver. This is not the case for everyone, however: I know people who relied on one or two special friends to be their caregivers. No matter how this person/these people are involved in your life, it's important to know who your caregiver is and to love and respect them while you're in treatment. Who is/are your caregiver(s), and how will you love them?

_____

_____

_____

Michael Holtz

Chapter 3: Stay Positive

*"Anyone can give up, it's the easiest thing in the world to do. But to hold it together when everyone else would understand if you fell apart, that's true strength." -- Chris Bradford, **The Way of the Sword***

I heard the words "You have cancer" on a Tuesday morning. Worst Tuesday ever, right? It could have been, I suppose. We were more than a little shell-shocked, to be sure. Neither of us had anticipated walking out of the endoscopy center that morning with a cancer diagnosis hanging over us. Yet Sarah and I knew things could be much, much worse.

"You know, I'm gonna be okay," I said when we were in the car. Our location in this moment was important to this conversation, so let me give you a little context: We were at a stoplight, headed to lunch as it had been somewhere around 30 hours since I'd ingested solid food of any kind. We were a block from the endoscopy center. At this corner, I could see the sign for the American Cancer Society, where I worked. Over 10 years of employment, I had met a lot of cancer survivors -- a lot. And I knew from the research we had conducted that survival rates from cancers of all kinds were on the rise while death rates from cancer were on the decline. We are, very slowly but also very surely, winning the war against cancer.

"We're going to get through this," I continued. "Something will kill me, but not cancer. Not this time."

Sarah nodded, believing completely that we were going get through this. Understand that we had only a diagnosis at this point. We didn't know the stage or have a treatment plan. The months ahead would be rough. My gastroenterologist, God bless him, said that in three or four months we'd be on the other side of cancer. Little did he know we were facing a very long 11 months.

At this point we, along with my gastroenterologist, were the only people who knew I had cancer. Calls would have to be made. People would have to be told: family, friends, co-workers and so on. This was going to take a lot of time and energy over the next few days.

By making the choice together to stay positive, we made a tacit agreement that negativity of any kind would not be tolerated -- by anyone. The imaginary conversation in my head went something like this: "Yes, I have cancer. No, I'm not going to die. Yes, treatment may be difficult. Yes, we're scared. We are staying positive through all of this. If you can't get with the program and be and stay positive for us, then we'll see you when it's over." Seriously, there would be no tolerance of negativity.

Of all the calls we made and conversations we had, there was only one close call: with my in-laws. They knew I had been having digestive issues and that I had a colonoscopy coming up. We had shared with them my concern that perhaps I had celiac disease so I was not eating bread or anything made from wheat. As a result, different arrangements would have to be made for my birthday cake. They reluctantly ordered a gluten-free carrot cake from the local health-food store.

We called to tell them the news.

"I was afraid of that," my mother-in-law said.

Really? I thought to myself. Even my learned gastroenterologist/Navy doctor/chief scoper to President Ronald Reagan wasn't expecting to tell me I had cancer. Without missing a beat, Sarah took up the positivity charge and let her parents know in no uncertain terms that negativity would not be accepted. If they wanted to be part of the journey, they would have to get their minds right about this.

You know what? They did. In fact, they were among our fiercest advocates and supporters during the entire experience. When I was in the hospital recovering from surgery, they spent part of two days in my hospital room. They didn't have to be entertained: they left me to recover. My mother-in-law read books; my father-in-law listened to birdcalls on his iPod. And my father-in-law is one of my biggest encouragers when it comes to this book project, because he saw firsthand the benefits of positivity and gratitude and surrounding yourself with good people and on and on.

Understand, I don't call out my in-laws here to make fun of them or criticize them -- not in the least. I adore my in-laws. I also understand that they grew up in a time when a cancer diagnosis was a death sentence and that they've lost several family members and friends to the disease. They have a completely different frame of reference about the disease than a guy who knows the disease statistics like the back of his hand.

I use the illustration of my in-laws' response to my cancer diagnosis simply to make the point that as cancer patients we have the right and responsibility to ourselves to set the limits for what is tolerated or not during our individual cancer experiences.

Not once did I ever ask the question "Why me?" It wouldn't have done any good. Also, like I said, I knew the statistics. One in every two men will be diagnosed with cancer in his lifetime, according to the American Cancer Society. So, why *not* me?

Understand that this wasn't a choice to be Pollyannaish and ignore the negatives of having cancer. We didn't yet know what to expect at all, yet we knew treatment would be difficult. And because we were still in the bubble of having a diagnosis but not yet having a treatment plan, we were very aware of the possibility that I could die.

Still, we held our heads high and pushed through. We believed with every fiber of our beings that God was in control and would take care of things, no matter the outcome. We were positive everything would be all right in the end. And, to paraphrase the saying, if it was not all right, it would not be the end.

Let me make one thing clear here: not once did I believe that having a positive attitude would slow or stop the spread or cure my cancer. While some people believe this and share anecdotal stories about how a positive mindset can lead to cancer cures, there is no credible research to back up such a claim. Rather, a positive attitude for us was a survival mechanism, a means to get through a very difficult situation without succumbing to depression or wallowing in negativity.

I also realize that I can speak only myself here. I was not diagnosed with terminal cancer. But I do know people whose diagnoses were far worse than mine yet who remained positive throughout more onerous treatments than I faced -- some even as they faced death.

Something else that was important to staying positive: I was very open about my cancer journey, with Sarah's blessing, of course. As a PR guy who worked for the American Cancer Society, I saw this as my opportunity to demystify a disease that scares the hell out of people. As a rule, unless they're porn stars, people don't like talking about what happens in the pelvic region of their body. I wanted to let people in on every step of the process.

I shared a lot on social media. My cancer journey is heavily documented on CaringBridge and Facebook. If you think for even a second that Facebook and other forms of social media are irrelevant, all you have to do is announce to the world that you have cancer. A whole separate community of support sprung up for us on Facebook during my months of treatment.

Because I am a PR guy and a fairly well-respected one in my community, a lot of my journey is documented in traditional media as well. There have been so many media stories in various forms – from features to op-eds and more -- that I began to feel like Knoxville's only living cancer survivor. Of course, I know that's not true, but apparently I give good quote.

I'm proud to say that the way I shared my journey served as a template of sorts for friends I know who were diagnosed after me. Kim Hansard, a dear friend and the co-host of *The Mark and Kim Show*, the morning drive show on Star 102.1 here in Knoxville, was diagnosed with breast cancer in October 2013, ironically the day after she co-hosted the American Cancer Society Making Strides Against Breast Cancer walk. When she was ready, she discussed her diagnosis on-air and on Facebook and shared very openly about her surgery, recovery and reconstruction.

We've talked several times, including a 30-minute interview on her radio group's public-service show, about how being open about our respective experiences has been a blessing not just to ourselves but to others. Sharing our experience indeed demystifies cancer, and I think we both believe it gives the people diagnosed after us hope for recovery and a great life on the other side of the disease.

One more thing here: consciously choosing to be positive didn't mean there were no bad days during cancer treatment. There certainly were those. My butt-crack felt like it had been severely sunburned by radiation therapy and actually blistered. Surgery left me in pain for weeks. There were days when chemotherapy left me unable to move. And colostomy appliance failures are simply a fact of my life now.

Over lunch one day, my pastor marveled at my ability to project positivity. She didn't doubt at all that it was real, because not only had she seen my positive posts on Facebook, she had also seen me in church. Still, she had a question for me.

"What happens when you have a shit day?" she asked (Lutheran pastors can get away with language like that).

"That's a day I don't post on Facebook," I replied.

Being positive is most certainly a choice for most people. We can decide for ourselves which emotions we bring to anything we are experiencing. Wallowing in negativity would have been easy, quite honestly. Cancer sucks. Treatment is hard. I'll shit in a bag for the rest of my life. Still, I choose to be positive.

After all, I'm still here.

Mindset Exercise

Being diagnosed with cancer or another serious illness is most certainly difficult, physically and psychologically. Still, even after diagnosis there are things in your life about which you can be positive, whether it's that you have a home, or a job, or a family member, or a dog who loves you unconditionally no matter how you feel. Name three things in your life right now about which you can be positive.

_____

_____

_____

Michael Holtz

Chapter 4: Be Grateful

"Gratitude turns what we have into enough, and more. It turns denial into acceptance, chaos into order, confusion into clarity ... it makes sense of our past, brings peace for today, and creates a vision for tomorrow." -- Melody Beattie

I would like to think that I've always been a grateful person.

I learned to say "thank you" early in my life. I have written thank-you notes for gifts received for birthdays, Christmases, graduation. I verbally thank people who do nice things for me, waitstaff who keep my iced-tea glass full, and so on. At Thanksgiving, I can always rattle off a list of the things for which and people for whom I am grateful.

During cancer, I discovered that expressing gratitude is one thing. Embodying gratitude, living a lifestyle of gratitude, if you will, is something else entirely. I made this discovery about halfway through chemotherapy, when I found a book that would strengthen my faith and change my life.

Let me say here that I have always been a voracious reader. I learned to read before kindergarten and really haven't stopped since. During cancer, I read something like 75 books, because reading was something that could fill the time spent in waiting rooms before doctor appointments, in the hospital recovering from surgery, in the chemotherapy lounge while drugs dripped into my port, and on the couch too fatigued to move.

One December day, in the throes of a mental fog caused by chemotherapy, I realized I had finished all the books in my stack and went searching on Sarah's bedside table for something to occupy my time and my mind. In her stack was *one thousand gifts*, by Ann Voskamp, a book given to Sarah by a print vendor she works with at her advertising agency.

One thousand gifts is indeed a book about gratitude. More important, Voskamp writes about gratitude during tough times: loss of a child, death of a parent, diagnosis of illness.

Voskamp writes about the concept of *Eucharisteo*. It's the Greek word that means "thanksgiving" or "to be grateful." She writes that God gives us gifts every day, but because many of them are small, we miss them. Her challenge to readers, and thus the title of her book, is to be intentional about discovering the gifts God gives us every day and write them down. On her website, www.aholyexperience.com, she offers daily prompts to help readers discover these gifts. Roughly three gifts a day, which comes out to one thousand gifts a year.

Have you ever been grateful for the play of colors when the sun shines on a sinkful of soapsuds, or the thud a pinecone makes when a child tosses it into a bucket, or the butterfly that flits by the window on its way to the garden? In Alice Walker's *The Color Purple*, one of the characters, Shug, puts it this way: "I think it pisses God off when you walk by the color purple in a field and don't notice it."

I don't know that it pisses God off when we don't notice, but I do believe that, as one of the songs in the movie says, "God is trying to tell us something."

In my favorite passage, Voskamp writes that "Eucharisteo -- thanksgiving -- always precedes the miracle." We see this every Sunday in Communion, when we remember the Last Supper. Jesus raises the bread and the wine, gives thanks to God and then tells us do this in remembrance of Him. He is crucified, and then there is the miracle of the Resurrection.

To explain my understanding of Eucharisteo always preceding the miracle, I want to take you back to the day of my surgery, August 10, 2012, a Friday.

The plan was relatively simple, as cancer surgeries go. My surgeon would go in, remove the tumor and then hook the disconnected sections of my colon back together.

Turns out it wasn't quite that simple. I was not present for any of this because I was high on drugs in the recovery room, but I know that my usually ebullient, smiling and upbeat surgeon was seriously downcast when he came into the waiting room to talk with Sarah, our family and our friends. The surgery was much more difficult than he'd anticipated, the tumor much larger than expected. Because of its size and the amount of scar tissue from radiation therapy, my entire rectum had to be removed, leaving me with a permanent colostomy.

Even more worrisome, he wasn't sure he'd gotten all the cancer. The male pelvis is a very tiny space, and the margins between the tumor and other organs were very, very small. He told the assembled group that everything would depend on the results of the pathology report: future treatment, future surgery, life or death -- everything.

We prayed for a good report, of course, but we were also very grateful. We were grateful for the amazingly gifted surgeon, for my medical team, even for the research that led to the development of the colostomy.

Three days later, while Pastor Amy was visiting with us, my surgeon practically floated into the room. He'd been pressing the pathologist for the report to the point that the pathologist called him in the middle of another surgeryto report that there were no living cancer cells in any of the tissue he examined.

No living cancer cells. The treatment worked.

I'm not embarrassed at all to report that I wept like a baby. After the doctor left, Sarah, Amy and I prayed though tears together, giving thanks to God. Then I cried some more. Gratitude did indeed precede the miracle.

Here's the epic part, the thing I learned about gratitude in all of this:

Eucharisteo is not just about noticing the color purple in a field, enjoying a piece of music or laughing over a joke and being grateful for those things. What *one thousand gifts* challenges us to do is practice the presence of God.

The simplest way for me to think of practicing the presence of God is to imagine living a monastic life. Monks and nuns live humbly and gratefully, their every need met through community. Someone is responsible for feeding the members of the order, another makes sure the larder is full, someone does laundry, if there is a farm, some members tend animals or grow crops, someone else may work in the gift shop, which brings in some of the money to buy the food that is prepared to sustain the community. All of this work and more is done by people whose hearts are filled with gratitude and who believe and pray as they're working that what they're doing is for the glory of God.

Most of us are not called to the monastic life, but we can practice the presence of God. Ann Voskamp shows us one way: by looking for and giving thanks for the gifts that are around us every day. God showers these gifts on us -- small things and big things -- to help us realize and know in our hearts and minds that He is with us. He's with us washing the dishes, or walking by a field, or driving to work, or facing the death of a family member. He is, as Isaiah prophesied and Matthew recalled, Emmanuel, "God with us." Come hell or high water, He is with us.

Gratitude -- embodying it, living it, and practicing it -- can change your perspective. It might even change your life. In fact, a whole body of scientific research proves exactly that.

Robert Emmons, PhD, is a pioneer in the study of gratitude and a professor of psychology at the University of California, Davis, where he is lead researcher at the university's Greater Good Science Center. Emmons conducts research on the impact gratitude has on emotional and psychological well-being, as well as on relationships.

Emmons's work demonstrates that expressing gratitude to the people -- whether partners, colleagues or friends -- who have done things for us we appreciate absolutely strengthens our relationships. "Lifestyle gratitude," which stems from the idea of keeping a gratitude journal and writing down three to five things every day for which you are grateful, improves our overall emotional well-being and makes us happier. In fact, happiness among people who practice lifestyle gratitude increases by as much as 25 percent. How much better would the world be if we were all 25 percent happier?

Voskamp spoke about the ability to increase happiness through gratitude at an event called the Cue Conference. A video of her talk is available online. Keeping a gratitude journal, she said, has a big impact on everyone, but in fact, the biggest impact is on men.

"It's the *men*!" she exclaimed when I, as one of few men daring enough to attend a women's Advent event in

December 2014, met her in person. She added that her publisher was about to release a duotone leather version of *one thousand gifts* so men wouldn't be embarrassed to be seen carrying a book with a bird's nest on the cover.

When it comes to getting through hard times, Emmons writes for dailygood.org that gratitude is essential because we have the most to gain by being grateful during a crisis, including energy, healing and hope.

"Trials and suffering can actually refine and deepen gratefulness if we allow them to show us not to take things for granted," he writes. "Our national holiday of gratitude, Thanksgiving, was born and grew out of hard times. The first Thanksgiving took place after nearly half the pilgrims died from a rough winter and year. It became a national holiday in 1863 in the middle of the Civil War and was moved to its current date in the 1930s following the Depression."

Does gratitude come easy during difficult times? Not at all. Emmons says it's easy to feel grateful during good times but much harder to tap into gratitude when someone has died, is sick, has lost a job, etc. It is important, however, to recognize that there is a difference between *feeling* grateful and *being* grateful. We cannot always control our emotions, but we can control our attitude in the face of difficulty. Gratitude is a choice. It gives us a perspective that life is long, relatively speaking, and that our present circumstances are temporary.

By practicing gratitude, in the same way we would practice mindfulness or yoga, we can prepare ourselves to be better equipped to face the difficulties that are inevitable in life.

Mindset Exercise

For the next seven days, practice lifestyle gratitude by sharing three things for which you are grateful every day. When the week is over, feel free to continue your list on the *Gratitude* app for iPhone or Android devices, in Ann Voskamp's *one thousand gifts* devotional journal or in a blank notebook.

Day One
1. _____

2. _____

3. _____

Day Two

1. _____

2. _____

3. _____

Day Three

1. _____

2. _____

3. _____

Day Four

1. _____

2. _____

3. _____

Day Five

1. _____

2. _____

3. _____

Day Six

1. _____

2. _____

3. _____

Day Seven

1. _____

2. _____

3. _____

Chapter 5: Be Loved

"When someone has cancer, the whole family and everyone who loves them does, too." -- Terri Clark

It would have been easy, I suppose, to distance myself from the rest of the world after hearing the words "You have cancer."

How and what cancer patients share is based on their comfort level. Some share their diagnosis with very few people, staying private about the day-to-day struggles of the experience. Others keep people at a distance out of concern that friends and family will worry needlessly. For still others, their sense of pride makes them refuse offers of help, even when help is needed.

I personally know of people who died of cancer, but no one in the world knew until after they passed away, because the individual kept the information so intensely private.

I understand the desire to keep everything close to the vest, but I knew at the outset that that approach wasn't going to work for me. Working for the American Cancer Society Cancer Action Network while having a cancer experience is anything but private. Also, as a public relations practitioner who knows a lot of people, I wouldn't have been able to keep the news under wraps for long. Ultimately, staying private about my diagnosis simply wasn't going to work for me.

As I mentioned in "Stay Positive," I was very open about my experience and shared much of it on social media. Facebook and CaringBridge, a website that connects patients with loved ones, were important tools in sharing my story. I also shared experiences on my blog.

Now, I didn't just jump on Facebook one day and start sharing. It was important that Sarah was comfortable with my being open about my journey, and I didn't share anything until we knew my young nieces and nephews who use Facebook had heard from their parents about my diagnosis. Beyond that, there were no ground rules: I could and did share everything, all from a positive perspective.

Social media proved a great means to share details with the most people. From oncology appointments to preparations for surgery to chemotherapy sessions, it was all out there. And my Facebook friends turned out in droves to support us. Messages of love and support poured in by the train-car load. It was amazing.

A more tangible means of support came from my colleagues at work. When I told my co-workers about my cancer diagnosis, they rallied around me. I positioned my cancer experience as the ultimate marathon and let them know that I needed them to ring cowbells to help propel me to the finish line.

They responded -- with cowbells. Cowbells of all shapes and sizes came in to my office, most of them painted with messages of support or Scripture verses. My friends Megan and Jenny organized the cowbell effort, and I am grateful for their support. Each cowbell is important, and some of them were of serious import and entrusted to my care. For example, one of my cowbells is from the drum kit of a jazz musician named Ian Wallace, who passed away from esophageal cancer caused by exposure to secondhand smoke in nightclubs. His wife, Marjorie, entrusted the cowbell to my care. Another, from fellow marathon runner David Pittman, was the cowbell his wife, Mary Jo, rang during every marathon he finished as an American Cancer Society athlete. Even Nate Farmer and the rest of the folks at Frank's Barbershop, my favorite place to get my hair cut, presented me with a cowbell when I got my hair cut before surgery.

There was a bit of a ceremonial aspect to the delivery of cowbells. My colleagues and friends in the Knoxville office volunteered to drive me to radiation treatment so Sarah didn't have to miss work every day to take me to treatment. When we returned to the office, anyone who was around would greet me with the clanging of cowbells as I walked in the door, and the "cowbell of the day" was presented. Cowbells continued after radiation therapy all the way to my first birthday after cancer treatment. That bell, which reads "Happy Cancer-Free Birthday, Michael," was signed by all my friends in the Knoxville office and remains a highly treasured item.

To help us out after I got home from the hospital, Megan organized meals for us. Friends from the office and from throughout the world of local public relations volunteered to cook meals for us. It was wonderful to have the opportunity to talk with different friends -- and to enjoy delicious food -- every day

I recommend every patient fighting a difficult illness get a Megan. She was invaluable in helping organize all of the people who wanted to "do something." Offers of help came out of the woodwork. It was amazing and humbling to be showered with so much love. I also recommend accepting those offers of help. Let people cook, clean, do the laundry, mow the yard, babysit the kids, etc. Fewer tasks for you and your caregiver means you can focus on getting well.

The Christian viewpoint on all of this has to do with blessings. If you turn down an offer for help, no matter how insignificant it may seem, you're blocking someone from being blessed by being part of your journey. The helper will be blessed, and you will be blessed -- and relieved -- by accepting the help.

For people who want to "do something," I give you permission to go ahead and do it. Don't ask if you can mow the lawn, or bring dinner, etc. Just do it. Neither the cancer patient nor the caregiver has the time or the energy to make sure all of the household chores get accomplished, unless they're intensely Type-A personalities. You will be helping. Just do it.

We also found incredible support from our church family, which was a beautiful thing because through the early part of my cancer experience, we weren't members of any church.

Sarah and I spent a few years floating among three Knoxville churches, including St. John's Lutheran Church, where we ultimately landed. We floated among the churches because we had grown disillusioned by our Southern Baptist megachurch. I was a leader in the church and a member of its very popular choir. When we disappeared from the church, though, we were barely missed. There were a couple of people who reached out and who remain dear friends to this day. But, by and large, it was as if we had never gone to that church.

We went in search of a new church home, but it wasn't as easy as finding our previous church. When we walked into the doors there, we both knew from the first moment that we were in the right place. This time around, though, we were divided. The nondenominational evangelical church we visited was nice, but it was too similar to the church we'd left. We liked the small urban hip church we visited often, but locking in on community was challenging. We liked the people at the Lutheran church, but it was a significant departure from Sarah's upbringing. Were we ever going to find agreement?

After my diagnosis, we had dinner with Pastor Amy Figg, who knew we were undecided about a church affiliation and urged us to consider St. John's Lutheran our church home, even if it was only "a soft place to land" during our cancer experience. So we became regular attendees at St. John's, and Sarah and Amy had several lovely conversations that allowed Sarah to work through concerns she had about the differences between Lutheran and Baptist theology and doctrine.

Ultimately, it was the realization that I could die during surgery that led us to become members of St. John's. I pulled the cancer card, quite honestly. I told Sarah that any obituary about me needed to say I was "a member" of a church, whether St. John's or elsewhere. So, a week before surgery, I called the Reverend Steve Misenheimer, our senior pastor, and asked whether it would be possible for us to join the church even though it wasn't the traditional time to do so. That Sunday, five days before surgery, we were welcomed into our new church family.

But the members of St. John's had been praying for us and offering support and encouragement long before the Sunday we joined the church. We were visited by pastors Steve, Amy and John Tirro while I was in the hospital. Prayers continued throughout chemotherapy, and as we got to know more people in the church, they became part of my social-media support community too. We are so grateful for our church family.

The support from our friends and family was also amazing. My mom, sister and niece came down from Wisconsin when I was in the hospital. My in-laws came to the hospital as well and regularly checked in on us.

Our friends were all over us in various ways. These are just a few of the examples:

• Tina kept close tabs on us, invited us out to dinner regularly and brought a huge box of cookies from the bakery where she works to the hospital for all of the guests who would converge during my stay.

• Duane, Kathy, Keith, Angie, Erin and Sherry came to the hospital for a visit a day or two after surgery. We got to laughing so hard, I was afraid I would pop my stitches.

• Zane, who was an acquaintance at the time but has become one of my dearest friends (more on that in another chapter), visited my hospital room the day we found out the great news about the pathology report.

- Missy, Mick, Georgia, Jodie, Janae and a passel of friends from high school I hadn't seen in more than 25 years sent a stack of supportive notes along with a cowbell.

- Jerry sent a prepublication copy of his book about his personal experience with a higher power.

- Our mailbox was flooded with cards and notes from friends, family, colleagues and even strangers who knew about my story from others.

The point of all of this is simple: Cancer is difficult. Love is all around you. People have it to give. Allow yourself to be loved. Being loved will help you through the experience.

Mindset Exercise

You are going to need help during your illness, whether with simple tasks around the house, childcare, petting-sitting, grocery shopping, etc. Two questions here: First, how are you willing to let people express their love for you (in other words, how can the people in your life help you during your illness)? Second, whom can you ask to take charge of organizing the help you need?

_____

_____

_____

_____

Michael Holtz

Chapter 6: Find Your Tribe

"When you find people who not only tolerate your quirks but celebrate them with cries of 'me too!' be sure to cherish them. Because those weirdos are your tribe." -- Anonymous

I cannot emphasize enough the importance of support we received during my cancer experience. My friends, family and co-workers were extremely supportive and helpful to Sarah and me, as I explained earlier. I also had the social-media community that rallied around us and offered encouragement on Facebook and CaringBridge. We needed all of that support, and then some.

While on a visit to Thompson Cancer Survival Center before I started chemotherapy, I saw a poster promoting a program for survivors offered by the Cancer Support Community of East Tennessee. I called about participating in the program but learned I had to complete treatment before I could participate. As I was still looking at six months of chemotherapy, I was definitely not a candidate. The person on the other end of the phone recommended I join CSC's support group for patients in active treatment and asked whether I was interested in coming in for an intake meeting with a counselor.

In the seven years of psychotherapy I had undergone earlier in my life, I had found the group-therapy process very helpful. So I agreed to come in for an intake session and joined the support group. Within a week, Sarah joined the CSC support group for caregivers.

You might think being in a roomful of people in the midst of cancer treatment would be a sad affair. You would be wrong. In addition to offering support, empathy and valuable inside information for our fellow cancer fighters, we often laughed our asses off.

As I learned during my journalism career, often the most raucous laughter emanates from the darkest places of the human experience. Many of the journalists I've met who work police beats and editors on the night shift have dark senses of humor. It's a coping mechanism for reporting on and writing about murder scenes, fatal car accidents and the like.

A similarly dark sense of humor helps when coping with cancer. Nothing, it seems, is funnier than vomiting like a volcano, being unable to drive because of medication or eating foods that all taste like the inside of a tin can as a result of chemotherapy side effects. Some of the best laughter came from my telling stories about colostomy failures. Shitting yourself is hilarious when you're talking about it as a past event.

"You're so funny when you talk about such a horrible thing" was something I heard almost every time I shared a colostomy-appliance failure tale.

We cursed, and laughed about cursing. Like laughter, cursing is a release, whether from the frustration of doctors who seemed dismissive of our concerns about treatment or side effects or because, sometimes, a well-placed curse word is the only appropriate thing you can say to a fellow group member who has been diagnosed with a recurrence. I'm pretty sure a dozen of us said "shit" when a group member reported her cancer had returned. Even worse were the words we used when someone was terminal or transitioning to hospice care. But even in those instances, it wasn't long before we were laughing again, sometimes through our tears.

We laughed often about unintentionally breaking a cardinal rule of group: no identifying specific physicians. Concealing our doctors' identities protected them from both direct criticism and favoritism. But it's difficult to remember not to use your doctor's name when talking about appointments and recommendations. So anytime someone let a doctor's name slip, we'd gasp in mock horror, then laugh about it.

We laughed about chemo ports that stopped working, blood draws that didn't take, caregivers who were afraid of losing us but afraid to talk about it. We laughed about the prospect of death, and we also attended the funeral services of group members who passed away. Losing group members was difficult for all of us, because it brought us face to face with the grim possibility of our own demise.

So we laughed in the face of death and pain and suffering. We empathized with each other as we shared how side effects from the chemotherapy and other drugs we were affecting our bodies and our minds.

More than anything, we understood each other. As cancer patients, we all knew what hearing the words "you have cancer" meant. We were all meeting with doctors, some of us getting second opinions. Most of us were undergoing treatment, some for the first time, some for the second or third. Others in the group had decided to stop treatment because it wasn't working or because their quality of life was so dramatically impacted by treatment, there was no quality in their life.

Not everything was illness focused, though. We also talked about our successes in the life outside of cancer, whether that meant running races for the first time since diagnosis or finishing a degree or having children. We even threw a baby shower for a member one night after the "official" group meeting had ended.

Wherever we were in our individual cancer experiences, we were on the journey together. We shared the frustration of long days in the chemotherapy infusion room and the challenge of being wiped out with fatigue. We talked about caregivers who were often overly attentive out of fear that something else was going to go wrong with us. Every aspect of the cancer experience was covered during the nearly two years I was a member of the group.

My group mates and I were very much a family, right down to our individual dysfunctions, and I will consider being in group one of the best parts of my cancer experience. Which made leaving group a very difficult decision.

At the time I decided to leave group, I was almost two years from my surgery and more than a year from finishing chemotherapy. I loved being in the group, but I knew in my heart it was time to make room for something completely unrelated to cancer. My world was almost entirely cancer focused, from working for the American Cancer Society Cancer Action Network to dealing with my colostomy appliance every day to wondering when my body was going to respond to all the working out I was doing (some of which had to be modified because of how cancer had ravaged my body). I knew I needed to start making room for a life beyond cancer, and leaving group was the first step in doing just that.

Leaving was difficult but necessary. Every once in a while, on a Monday night, I wonder how the meeting is going.

In addition to support groups, the Cancer Support Community of East Tennessee offers a number of programs for cancer patients and their families, including yoga, mindfulness meditation for stress release, cooking demonstrations, music therapy, information sessions about cancer research and treatment, and art classes.

It was in the first art class I'd ever attended, on a sunny Friday afternoon, that I met two members of my tribe, Belinda and Kim, or Bart and Kart. My nickname was Mart. As you can see, we added the first initials of our names to the word "art" to derive our nicknames. Silly, but fun.

Belinda was in treatment for ovarian cancer when I met her, and Kim her best friend and supporter. We found ourselves together at the end of a very long table on the day we were making jewelry, if I recall correctly. We laughed and joked around and became fast friends, the Three Musketeers of art class. I made new friends and made Sarah a pair of dangly earrings. It was a good day.

We're in regular contact, Bart, Kart and I. We meet for coffee or cheesecake from time to time. We've participated in Relay for Life together. We've walked Buddy's Race Against Cancer together. When Stand Up to Cancer and the American Cancer Society joined forces in September 2014, we attended the viewing party together.

And, as cancer patients and survivors are wont to do, Belinda and I clicked on a bit of a different level. She came to my office after an appointment with her doctor. She had been diagnosed with a recurrence, only this time the tumor was in a place that couldn't be reached surgically. She could be treated, but if it didn't work to keep the tumor in check, she might have to receive treatment on and off for the rest of her life.

"What would you do?" she asked, on the verge of tears.

How do you answer that question? I was a survivor finished with treatment at this point, but any answer I gave would be purely hypothetical. At the end of the day, though, I would want at least to try something and see how much time elapsed between the end of the next round of treatment and subsequent recurrence, if it came, then make a decision about treating again. Along the lines of a 12-step program, you focus on doing the next right thing, not on the entire journey that lies ahead.

I don't know if my opinion helped or not, but Belinda decided to do treatment again, and then again after that only if, on the second time through, the doctor could guarantee she wouldn't lose her hair again. Apparently he could make that guarantee, and Belinda's still here and still being treated.

One of my favorite tribes is my running tribe. In addition to training for and running marathons and half-marathons, I have volunteered many, many times for races throughout my community. I've worked water stops, been a course monitor, registration chair and race director. I was race director for one of the largest and longest-held races in Knoxville, the Expo 10K and 5K, during my cancer year, specifically during radiation treatment in late May.

In fact, on the Friday before the race, I went directly from lying flat on the linear accelerator to the Knoxville Civic Coliseum, where the race has been held for many years. We needed to unload cases of water from our television sponsor's van onto a dolly and into storage. I felt good and wanted to help as much as possible. Bill Evans, then community relations director for the television station, stopped me when he realized I'd just come from treatment. During the event the next day, I admit I didn't move a whole lot. It was hot and humid, and I was near the end of treatment, so I was tired. Sarah helped me hand out race awards at the conclusion of the race.

I love my running community. No matter your shape, experience or speed, most runners in Knoxville embrace you, something I learned earlier that year when I was asked to be social-media director for the Covenant Health Knoxville Marathon. Jason Altman, who is the race director and also a great friend, asked if I was interested. I jumped at the chance, and for weeks leading up to the race, I posted photos from the course, of directional arrows painted on the streets and more.

It was at the race expo the day before the event that I felt the warm embrace of my running community. I walked into the event and saw tons of friends and acquaintances, many of whom knew about my diagnosis and treatment, and all of whom wanted to talk to me or give me a big hug. From the "Sick Chicks," my running buddies from the Fleet Feet Knoxville marathon training program to my friends from the Covenant Health media team and the many, many volunteers I'd had the pleasure to work alongside for years, I got to see them all. It was like the return of the prodigal son.

When I relayed the story of feeling so welcomed to my friend Kristy Altman, who also happens to be Jason's wife, I was so overcome by the emotion of what had happened that day that I cried. She cried too, because she felt a similar sense of welcome after having stepped away from running for a bit to have their second child.

I must have done a good job with the race's social media, because Jason asked me to be social-media director again for the 2014 event. The cool thing about this race was that Mercedes-Benz of Knoxville was sponsoring the pace car, Mayor Madeline Rogero was going to ride in the pace car, and, as I learned later, my friend Zane wanted to make sure I was in the car as well.

I was extraordinarily stoked. I was going to ride a pace car -- with the mayor and Lee Ann Furrow Tolsma, co-owner of the dealership. It was my job to shoot photos of the awesome community supporters, bands, signs, cheer stations and volunteers along the course. A shot or two of the pack leaders wouldn't hurt either. In short, this was going to be fun. Only it almost didn't happen, thanks to my colostomy.

There I was, 15 minutes before the start of the marathon, surrounded by members of the Mercedes-Benz of Knoxville Marathon Team, getting our pictures taken around a gorgeous convertible, when I felt my colostomy appliance give way. It's a feeling I can only describe as a sudden awareness of a sticky wetness on my left hip. I was about to seriously crap myself. I needed to change my appliance, and fast, but where and how?

I was too far away from the long line of porta-potties on the other side of the starting line to get there and back. The starting line was on the Clinch Avenue bridge, above World's Fair Park. It occurred to me I could dash down the stairs to the restrooms just below the bridge.

I made a beeline for the men's room, which had two stalls. On this morning one of them didn't have a door. Fantastic.

I'm not sure if he saw distress in my eyes, but my friend Monty Howard was in front of me. He let me jump in ahead of him. And then I asked him to block the door for me because, well, it was about to get really weird. It's one thing to see a guy sitting on the toilet doing his business, it's entirely another to see a guy wiping his business from the left side of his abdomen.

I began frantically pulling medical supplies out of my backpack so I could switch out my appliance, only there was nowhere to put anything. No tiny shelf, no wide toilet paper holder, no nothing. This was going to be a challenge.

I ultimately got myself cleaned up and began preparing a wafer -- the piece that adheres to my skin -- for placement around my stoma. In the process of applying adhesive, I dropped the thing into the toilet.

Shit.

Thank goodness I'd packed an extra.

I got the appliance in place, and then I had to strip because my boxer shorts were soiled.

At this point, Monty had to go because, well, he had to go -- and the race was about to start. I don't even know what time it was. Over the sound of my heart pounding in my ears, I think I heard "The Star-Spangled Banner." The starting gun would fire in mere moments. I had to hurry.

I swept up everything in my arms -- the boxers I was about to toss, the wrappers from my appliance, other trash that was on the floor of the stall -- and headed toward the trashcan and then the door.

I dashed up the stairs just in time to see the hand-cyclists roll past. I was certain the pace car had left without me. Gloriously, it had not. The mayor and Lee Ann were joined by David Luttrell, photographer extraordinaire, who was going to shoot photos for the first seven miles.

I jumped in, and off we went on what turned out to be a pretty incredible adventure.

No one was the wiser at that point, except Zane, whom I had texted on my way down and then back up the stairs, until I wrote a blog post about it. Jason still laughs about my colostomy failure story and nearly pooping on the mayor and a Mercedes in one shot. So did the members of my support group when I relayed the story to them the following Monday night.

That's why we need our tribes, so we offer mutual support, have someone to cry with or someone to laugh with through all of life's circumstances. If you don't have one, and I'm almost certain you do, I urge you to find your tribe. There's a great group of people out there waiting for you to join them.

Michael Holtz

Mindset Exercise

Our tribes are the groups of people we gravitate toward because we see them often, like our co-workers or our fellow parishioners at church, or because we have something in common, like a support group or exercise class. Where might you find your tribes?

_____

_____

_____

Michael Holtz

Chapter 7 - Use Your Words

"Most important thought, if you love someone, tell him or her, for you never know what tomorrow may have in store."
-- Walter Payton

People you know and love will do nice things for you during your cancer experience, if you let them. They might cook dinner, drive you to an appointment, mow the lawn, sit by your side during chemotherapy, or encourage you to think about the great life you're going to have on the other side of your illness.

Tell them how much you appreciate them.

Expressing gratitude for the things people do and telling those closest to me how much they mean to me has become very important to me and something I do on a regular basis. Some of my guy friends, in particular, might be uncomfortable with this, and that is never my intention, but in the event something happens and I die unexpectedly, I don't want to leave behind any doubt.

It likely stems from the dysfunctional relationship my dad and I had. I can honestly say I don't remember that he ever told me he loved me or was proud of me. On the night my dad died, his best friend sat on our couch and told my brothers, my sister and me how proud my dad was of us and how he talked about us all the time when he was on a deer-hunting expedition with the guys.

In my heart, I knew it couldn't be true. Why would he tell everyone else in his life but not the person he claimed to love? I didn't understand it, and I didn't buy it. I still don't.

My mom and other relatives are certain my dad loved me and have told me he did, but he never used the words. Not to me. And given the long standing difficulty in our relationship, anyone else's words are of little solace.

So I express my gratitude, and I tell the people I love that I love them.

In particular, I'm a big fan of the handwritten note. Don't get me wrong: I love receiving emails and texts of love and appreciation, and I love sending them too. But a handwritten note is like getting a piece of someone's heart. Sending a handwritten note allows me to express whatever I'm feeling in my own words. All of the cards and notes, and even emails, I received during my cancer experience -- I still have every single one of them in a basket. If ever I'm feeling down, I can go back and read those notes containing their healing words of love and encouragement.

I will say, on behalf of cancer patients everywhere that the people who do nice things for you while you are in treatment do not expect you to send them a thank-you note for every little thing you do. For example, if someone brings you dinner on Monday, you are not required to drop a thank-you note in the mail the next day. Tell them verbally you appreciate it. If you're active on social media, thank them on Facebook. Send a handwritten note later if you choose to do so.

Your job during treatment is to get well. Your loved ones who do nice things understand that. If you write a note every time someone does a nice thing while you are in treatment, you'll exhaust yourself. You have to focus on getting well.

I talked about, and posted on social media about, gratitude so often during my cancer experience that I incorporated gratitude into my spiritual practice during the 2013 Lenten season. Lent, for those unfamiliar, is the period of time between Ash Wednesday and Easter, which, in part, marks the period of time Jesus spent fasting in the wilderness before His triumphal entry into Jerusalem and subsequent crucifixion.

Many Christians observe Lent by given up something they see as an idol in their life, like coffee, chocolate, television or even social-media use.

That first Lent after cancer treatment, I decided to add sending notes of gratitude to my spiritual practice. Every day between Ash Wednesday and Easter, I wrote a note to someone in my life, whether family member, church member, colleague or friend. Each note included a basic statement of gratitude and an example of something they did or said for which I was grateful. I think it's important to tell why you're grateful.

I enjoyed the practice so much, I did the same thing in 2014.

Similarly, I think it's not enough just to tell someone they mean a lot to you or that you love them: it's also important to tell them why. What impact has the individual had on your life, specifically? Do you appreciate their encouragement and support? Did their very presence change your way of thinking about life in some profound way?

Tell them. Use your words. I promise you, your words will have an impact on the lives of the people you love.

Mindset Exercise

We should tell the people in our lives we love and appreciate them, and express thanks for things they've done for us. To whom do you need to share your words, and what would you say or write?

_____

_____

_____

Chapter 8: Be Open

"There are only two ways to live your life. One is as though nothing is a miracle. The other is as though everything is a miracle." -- Albert Einstein

I've already written about how gratitude helped get me through my cancer experience. Gratitude as a spiritual practice, a habit even, will always be part of my life, as will other spiritual practices, like prayer, meditation, worship at church and in private, even yoga and acupuncture.

I believe experiences like cancer and other difficult situations open a doorway between us and God (Heaven, the universe, Nirvana, whatever you choose to call it). Like millions of other cancer patients, Sarah and I leaned on our church family, friends and family who hold similar beliefs, and our existing spiritual practices to get us through the most difficult year of our lives together. We even took a mindfulness meditation class at the Cancer Support Community of East Tennessee together as a means of expanding the tools in our spiritual toolkit. While I admire people who can practice mindfulness, it takes a great deal of time and the ability to stay awake during practice. In short, we became meditation dropouts. Still, our experience with mindfulness meditation meant we were open to new spiritual experiences.

I've been a spiritual seeker for much of my life. I grew up in what I've always called a nonpracticing Catholic home. Mom was Catholic and dad was Lutheran, which was akin to being either a Shark or a Jet from *West Side Story*. Mom wrestled three little boys to church, where we sat behind thick glass in what Sacred Heart Catholic Church called their "crying room." But getting three little boy dressed and out the door was difficult and certainly didn't keep Mom in a frame of mind appropriate for church, and Dad didn't attend unless it was Christmas Eve or Easter morning, so she didn't have anyone to help her.

Something in me knew there was something bigger at work in the universe, though, so as I got older I continued to explore. An African-American friend invited me to his family' AME church. I loved going to his church, where there was soulful singing and impassioned preaching. In college, I spent several weeks visiting the School of Metaphysics, where a woman named Joyce dripped with crystals and big bangle bracelets and talked about astral planes and being light in the universe.

When I moved to Knoxville, I wanted to find a church home and became a regular attendee at a large United Methodist church near campus. When Sarah and I got married, we became members of a very large Southern Baptist megachurch. Then, when it was clear we needed something else, we settled on St. John's, an Evangelical Lutheran Church of America church on the edge of our city's mission district.

In the end, I don't believe one single denomination, or even one brand of religion, has a corner on the spirituality market: Eastern spirituality can enhance Western religions, and vice versa.

With that in mind, I'd like to explain three episodes from my cancer experience. In the first experience, my late father came to me in a dream.

Dad's appearance in my dream was quite a surprise. When he passed away in December of 1990, we were in the process of repairing what had been a very contentious and difficult relationship. There were a lot of words left unsaid and a lot of things left undone. This will sound cold, I know, but our relationship had been so strained that I was relieved by his passing.

We were like oil and water from early on. He was a high school football player, firefighter on a Navy aircraft carrier, car enthusiast, hunter, factory worker. I was an honor roll student, aspiring journalist, tuba player, and nerd. He didn't understand me, and I didn't understand him. Not that we didn't try.

He took me along once during deer-hunting season with a group of his buddies to Northern Wisconsin. Sitting quietly in the cold while holding a rifle and waiting for a deer to pass within range was incredibly boring. Then where was the drinking: I was too young to imbibe, but my dad and his buddies got plastered while eating greasy food like bratwursts and potato chips. Beer and bad food led to my nearly being gassed out of the trailer by the flatulence this group of men expelled. It was a long, stinky, bad weekend. I never went deer hunting again after that.

He clearly tried on occasion to treat me like I actually was his son, but most of the time he was angry with me. If I did or said something he didn't like, Dad would ignore me. And not just for short periods of time: there were times he would not speak to me or acknowledge my presence in the same room for months at a time.

Dad was critical of my weight, my intelligence, my friends, my striving to be the best person I could be. Being on the honor roll, getting letters to the editor published in the paper, even graduating from high school were not things to be celebrated. They were weapons used against me. In his mind, I thought I was too good for the family into which I'd been born.

Even so, there were rare moments of tenderness.

During my senior year of high school, I applied to and got accepted into journalism school at the University of Minnesota in Minneapolis. It was a dream come true. I loved the city, and the university had a great program. Dad didn't want me to go, though. In spite of our long contentious relationship, he asked me to go to college closer to home. So I gave up the dream and did my undergraduate work at the University of Wisconsin-Milwaukee, which was just a 45-minute commute from home. I don't begrudge that decision for a moment. I made wonderful friends and had a great college experience.

I was also close to home when dad had a heart attack that required sextuple bypass surgery at age 46 and also when he died two-and-a-half years later. We pledged to resolve our differences in the ICU after his surgery, but time was not on our side.

It took seven years of therapy and intentional work to reach a point of forgiveness, both of my father and myself. My therapist, one of the best men I have ever known, encouraged me to write my dad a letter expressing how I had been hurt and that, ultimately, I forgave him. I wasn't terribly keen on the idea. Then one night, while on a business trip, I swear I heard the voice of God tell me it was time to let it all go. It was time to forgive.

I sat at my laptop in the middle of the night and cranked out a six-page letter, listing the painful memories and also letting him know that I loved him and forgave him. A few weeks later -- on my birthday, in fact -- I was in Wisconsin visiting my family. I went to the cemetery and read the letter over his grave.

Forgiveness is not an instant process. There was no instant removal of all the pain. Rather, the letter was an important starting point. All these years later, I am mindful that we had a difficult relationship, but I am no longer pained by it. I even feel a great deal of empathy for my dad, because I have since learned that his relationship with my grandfather was equally difficult.

Still, it was a surprise to encounter him in my dream.

It was a wordless exchange. We were in a nondescript room, something along the lines of a medical office. We looked at each other. I sensed he knew about my diagnosis and wanted me to know he was around. There was no anger between us, no tension whatsoever, just an incredible sense of peace. As soon as I recognized that the tension I expected wasn't there, Dad disappeared. Then I woke up.

I still vividly remember that dream, though, and carry the peace it brought in my heart. Wherever my dad is now, I hope he's proud of the man I've become.

The second experience came during treatment when, at the urging of Andrew in my support group, I went to a healing-touch session. Lynn Anderson, a former nurse, is a healing-touch practitioner at Thompson Cancer Survival Center. The center's foundation provides funding for her salary so patients can be offered healing touch at no charge.

It's easier to explain what healing touch is not. For example, it is not massage. Rather, it's a form of energy therapy, and the practitioner redistributes the flow of energy around the cancer patient -- in this case, with intentional hand placements to help with long-term healing of the body.

I would lie fully clothed on a massage table while Lynn did her work. I swear to you, I could feel the transfer of energy from her body into mine. She would often talk about being rooted in the ground so that energy would flow up from the earth, through her and to me. Over time, this energy flow helped me feel less fatigued, and I even felt the neuropathy in my feet a little less. Healing touch was also very relaxing. I highly recommend healing touch to anyone who has the opportunity to have the experience for themselves.

The third experience I want to share came more than a year after cancer treatment, when I was being treated for neuropathy by an acupuncture practitioner named Joel Packard.

Joel and I had some amazing conversations, while I was lying on his acupuncture table, about karma and Buddhism, and being open to the workings of the universe, and visions. I had regular visions, during acupuncture sessions, of looking through a tiny window of what I'm certain was a Buddhist monastery, watching monks in rice-paddy hats working the fields. When I started acupuncture, the window appeared to be very tiny, but I could identify what I was seeing through the glass. As I continued, the window got larger and closer.

While the window is certainly a spiritual experience, that's not the end of it. The highlight of my acupuncture experience came toward the end, in my second-to-last session with Joel before he moved with his girlfriend to New Mexico.

After I had stripped and was lying on the table, looking like a combination porcupine and pincushion, Joel asked a startling but important question.

"What do you think was the spiritual cause of your cancer?"

I paused. I wasn't quite sure what he was getting at, but I had been his patient for the better part of a year. Not unlike the trust I feel for my surgeon, I trusted Joel. He seemed to sense my hesitation.

"For example, I had a patient who had problems in her pelvic region that she could relate back to being molested as a child."

My pause continued, and then: "Funny you should mention being molested," I started, and then let it all spill out:

Sadly, the most vivid memory of my childhood is that of being raped by a neighbor. His name was Paul. He was maybe 17 at the time. I was 5. He was the kind of guy every kid in the neighborhood admired, and he loved the kids in the neighborhood, especially my brothers and me.

He was the son of Cuban immigrants who lived in the house across the driveway from ours. He was gregarious and funny, and I trusted him implicitly. Which is why I didn't question him the day he found me alone in our backyard and asked me to follow him into his house.

Once we were inside, he led me into the living room. I remember hearing Spanish at a very loud volume on the television. I don't remember how I ended up naked on my stomach on the floor with him on top of me. I remember that it was very painful and that when he was finished, he rolled over, zipped up his pants, threatened to hurt me if I told anyone, and left the room. Feeling like I had to move my bowels, I went to the bathroom.

I got dressed and shakily walked back across the driveway. As I walked up the steps of our porch, I heard my mom on the phone. I stood in the kitchen, completely dazed and probably in shock. I watched my mom, who was talking and cooking and not paying any attention to the child in her midst.

I am certain that this experience was the beginning of the rift in my relationship with my dad. Ordinarily, when Dad got home from work, he would wrestle with us boys on the living room floor. That night, however, I wanted nothing to do with wrestling. Dad's opening move was a little too close to how Paul felt being on top of me. I cried. Loudly. I didn't want to wrestle, and I made that fact very clear.

No one asked what was wrong, or why I was pitching a fit. Honestly, given the threat Paul made, I probably wouldn't have told them if they had asked. And I didn't entirely understand what had happened. I did understand that it was bad and it was painful. Thus, I didn't want to be put in a position where it might be repeated. Dad and I never wrestled again. He was angry at me for this seeming act of rejection, but we never talked about it. Instead, the rift that opened up that night grew into a giant chasm between us.

Seventeen years passed before I ever talked about what Paul did to me. I wrote about it in a column for my college newspaper. The subject was the disbelief swirling around Professor Anita Hill's allegations of sexual misconduct against Supreme Court nominee Clarence Thomas. There were big questions about the amount of time that had passed between the alleged events and her reporting of them. The thesis of my column was that if you didn't believe Anita Hill, you couldn't believe me either.

By the time I wrote that column, Paul had been dead for several years. He shot himself in the head while sitting in his pickup truck. The karmic believer in me wants to think that maybe the guilt of his actions to me and likely to other children caught up to him.

Joel was crying when I finished sharing my story, and he thanked me for trusting him. I was still on the table, acupuncture needles strategically placed over my body, coming to the realization that my encounter with Paul could indeed have been the root cause of my cancer from a spiritual perspective.

"Not only did you have this traumatic experience, but you sat on it, literally and figuratively, for almost 20 years before were able to talk about it, and for even more years before you could forgive both Paul and your dad. All of that could create a very large tumor," he said.

Joel asked me to visualize healing light emanating from my gut and flowing through my colon -- not the one I have now, but that I should visualize a completely intact digestive system and follow the light around and through my gut.

I could see it. First as a red light, as if a laser were flowing through my body. The longer I visualized, the more the light changed, from red to blue to white. "Let the white light flood your body and beyond," Joel said, standing over me and massaging my temples and my forehead. "Let the light flow out of the top of your head and the bottoms of your feet, connecting to the healing energy of the universe."

I could see the light. I could even feel it. I could visualize a complete and healed body, no surgery, no colostomy bag. The sad part was, the visualization had to come to an end, and I arose from the table as I had come in -- a rectal-cancer survivor with a colostomy whose body had been ravaged by disease and surgery. Still, something was different. I was healed on a spiritual, psychic level.

Joel and I hugged. We laughed over the fact that the session had taken an interesting and difficult turn, but we were both grateful for the experience. From time to time I use the visualization technique I learned on the acupuncture table that day. I visualize my body whole and intact. One day I will be reunited with my complete spiritual body when I pass from this world to the next. While I'm not in a hurry to get there, I look forward to that day.

Mindset Exercise

Being open might mean giving yourself over to new and unfamiliar experiences, like yoga, healing touch, massage, acupuncture and mindfulness meditation. If you had to pick two, whether on the list above or not, what are you open to trying?

_____

_____

Chapter 9: Let Go

"Some of us think holding on makes us strong; but sometimes it is letting go." -- Herman Hesse

While a ubiquitous Disney movie pop anthem would have you believe that it's easy to "let it go," the reality is that it can be very difficult.

We human beings tend to resist change. Letting go means embracing change, whether it is a change we anticipated or one that was forced upon us as a result of facing an illness or simply living our daily lives. Change happens, whether we like it or not, which means the act of letting go becomes a necessary action. Whether or not you have experienced cancer is immaterial here, but because of my cancer experience, I realized I had to let go of three things: my dignity, some friends and, ultimately, my job.

The first thing I had to let go was my dignity. It comes with the territory for rectal-cancer patients, I suspect. Most every examination and test I underwent after diagnosis involved inserting something up my backside. Almost as bad was "the prep" that went along with those tests; disgusting concoctions of various laxatives and bowel cleaners to clear the way for a good scope or endoscopic ultrasound or flexible sigmoidoscopy.

The flex sig, by the way, is the only one of the procedures I had that didn't involve being knocked out with drugs. I was awake the entire time as my surgeon snaked the lower end of my colon. We talked about marathons and triathlons while I writhed on the table, grunting out answers about my own marathon experiences. I adore my surgeon, and he literally saved my life, so he gets a pass on the snake job.

My backside was tattooed with Sharpies in preparation for radiation therapy, three Xs to mark the spots where radiation would enter my body and, we hoped, kill the cancer. Every day for 28 days, I was required to bare my ass so the techs could fire their machine at those Xs. Twenty-seven times I checked in by giving my name and my birthdate to a tech who was checking my information against a computer screen that displayed a photograph of my face.

One time, a picture of my own tattooed ass was staring back at me when I checked in. The tech apologized profusely. It was an honest mistake, but I wondered if I was supposed to pull my pants down in that hallway.

A fabulous side effect to radiation therapy of the rectum is incontinence. It only happened a couple of times, but it was a couple times too many. I'd be out in the yard letting our dog do her business when I'd be overcome by the need to go myself. Twice that I recall, and there may be more, I didn't even make it into the house. Nothing makes me feel more enfeebled and helpless that crapping myself.

That's a feeling that continues now that I live with a permanent colostomy. While I've never exactly forgotten that I have a colostomy, most days I don't spend a lot of time thinking about it. My colostomy is part of my life and doesn't keep me from doing much of anything, including obstacle-course racing, jumping into the frigid Tennessee River for charity or joining in boot-camp-style workouts at my gym.

A colostomy blowout is a haunting experience. I had my first in the hospital, a day or two after surgery, because nurses used the wrong type of appliance for my body type. One of my worst blowouts, though, happened minutes before I was to share my cancer story at a public event about four months after surgery. There I was, talking to the event's public relations guy, when I felt a hot wetness in the area of my left hip. I was slated to be the first speaker at the event, and I was in trouble -- big trouble. I needed to change not only the appliance but my clothes as well.

As luck would have it, I had a change of clothes with me -- in my suitcase, which was in my car, which was in the parking garage. If I left to retrieve my bag, I would drip shit all over the hospital where the event was being held, which was not good from either a public health or clean-up perspective. I had to call a friend, who was in the meeting room for my talk, and ask her to come to the men's room, get my car key, then go to my car, get the bag and bring it to me so I could change my clothes.

Just a few minutes passed, but waiting while my lower body was slowly being covered in shit felt like an eternity. My friend knocked on the bathroom door; I stuck my arm out, grabbed the bag, and then went about the business of cleaning myself off. Standing stark naked in a very public hospital restroom, I realized I could have used a hose, but I had to make do with tap water and paper towels. The only other people who used the restroom while I was in there were hospital personnel who either understood what I was doing or were not at all surprised to see a fat, shit-covered naked guy standing in the middle of the room.

All of this occurred in the span of about 10 minutes, during which I got myself cleaned up, popped on a fresh appliance, dressed in my spare clothes and stuffed the soiled outfit into my bag, then headed into the meeting room just in time to be called to the stage. Except for worrying that I smelled like a sewage-treatment plant during the question-and-answer period, the event went off without a hitch.

While major blowouts, or "code brown" situations, are infrequent, they do occur. Afterward, I'm very likely to laugh about the situation and write about it on my blog. I hope to live a long life, which means there are any number of blowouts in my future. In the midst of them, though, I'm a mess both physically and emotionally as I work to get myself, and sometimes my surroundings, cleaned up.

Not everyone on earth, and in your world specifically, is equipped to handle difficult situations, like your cancer diagnosis. And some people may be there for part of the journey but disappear for the more difficult bits.

I tell people when I talk about my experience that if I'd had a "family portrait" of my friends before and after cancer, some of the faces would change. Many of those friends would appear in both portraits, and there would be a few new faces of friends who were maybe acquaintances but stepped up and stepped in to help or visit or call. But a few of the friends from the first portrait would be gone. Perhaps they were there and maybe even extremely helpful in the early stages of treatment, but because cancer treatment isn't always a short-term phenomenon or because your experience is too much a reminder of a loved one's cancer journey or because their circumstances have changed or for any other reason, they disappear.

Forgive them. After all, they're only human. I realize that sounds like a platitude, and I would like to tell you that it's easy, but it's certainly not that.

My example of letting friends go involves two friends I met in grad school. We were a bit like the Three Musketeers, and then Four when my lovely girlfriend came on the scene. They coupled up, got married, and had a kid, the whole schmear. Sarah and I also coupled up and got married. *Sans* kids we stayed focused on work. While our lives were different, we kept in pretty close touch through the years: dinners, outings, Christmas and birthday cards, and emails. There were times we felt more closely connected than others, but there always was a connection.

When I was diagnosed, they were among the first people I called. I knew the call could be fraught with challenges as the wife had lost her mother to cancer a few years earlier. I called anyway. We had a great conversation, and, as most people did, she offered to help in any way she could. It was a lovely conversation

And she lived up to her promise. I've said elsewhere that I played the cancer card to get our amazing dog, Marley. After we adopted her, we took her to visit our friends, or they came to us, and they were smitten with her. They loved her, their daughter loved her, and their dog loved her. We hung out a little more often because our dogs loved to play together, and we loved to watch them tear around the yard, chasing each other in big wide circles.

When I started chemo, they made this amazing offer: every Wednesday morning before my appointment, she would pick up Marley for the day, then bring her back in the afternoon when we returned from the treatment center. It was a beautiful arrangement that lasted through three months of chemo.

Then their dog had some form of behavior problem. Their dog trainer recommended he be kept away from other dogs until the problem could be resolved, which meant no more day trips for Marley. We certainly could make other arrangements for chemo days, but this was a beautiful arrangement for a dog everyone loved. As dog people ourselves, though, we understood. A few weeks later, I attempted to check in to see how their dog was doing. I heard not a word.

Two years later, and we haven't heard anything from them beyond a random group email inviting all of us to an event at their church.

I get it, truly I do. I think. Chemo has a cumulative effect on the human body. When we last saw them, I was in the middle of 12 rounds. I was already seriously fatigued, and it was only going to get worse. Maybe she couldn't handle seeing me get worse every other week. Or, conversely, because fatigue was the only real side effect I experienced during chemo, perhaps I didn't appear sick enough, so why was she bothering to take care of our Marley?

I don't know why, but I do know that I have forgiven them. And as I said earlier, I gained some friends during my cancer experience. My closest friend is someone I barely knew when I was diagnosed. Now we're invested in each other's life, we work together, we ran a business together, and we talk or text often. In the end, it was a good trade-off.

Two-and-a-half years after my cancer diagnosis, I left my job. Leaving the American Cancer Society Cancer Action Network was one of the most difficult decisions of my life. I'd worked for the organizations of the American Cancer Society for over 12 years. I was invested heart, mind and soul in the mission of eliminating cancer as a major health problem. I did some of the best work of my career for the organization.

But I was exhausted. Not by the work, but by the idea of spending another day completely submerged in the world of cancer. After a difficult year of fighting the disease -- and still working, by the way -- I continued to spend every day talking about cancer, specifically about legislation that could be passed in one of the 14 state I covered that would reduce the cancer burden.

I started feeling this malaise in February of 2014. It took me three months of self-reflection to determine what was behind the feelings of dread I experienced at the thought of going to work, and being tired of talking about cancer made perfect sense.

I decided to be open about what I was feeling, as I had been with much of my cancer experience, and reached out to my boss to have a conversation about it. Robert was supportive and understanding, and he ultimately said the organization would do just about anything to keep me because I was good at my job and highly respected by others. But there wasn't anything that could be done. This wasn't bucking for a raise or additional staff, although I certainly could have used both. There was a bigger force at play here: I was just plain tired of talking about cancer.

"Maybe you need to take a long vacation. I know you have plenty of time off coming to you."

It was a good thought, but the timing was bad. I was relatively new in my role, and planning was under way for the next legislative session. There was too much work to do, and there was only one other person on my team. I was already planning to take a vacation in July, so I added a couple of long weekends as well.

I was hopeful a few days off, even at sporadic intervals, would help. At this point, I hadn't decided it was necessary to leave. I wanted to get my mojo back. I reflected on some of the best work I had done, like the summer of 2011 when I organized or help stage more than 25 federal legislation-focused events across six states. I loved that summer. I didn't sleep much, and I was on the road a lot, but it was a wonderful time. That work also led to my being named ACS CAN's National Grassroots Professional of the Year in 2012 and then reawarded in 2013 because I missed the national meeting where the award was presented to recover from my cancer surgery.

The more I kept working, though, the worse the feeling of malaise got. I didn't want to do the work I was doing any more, not because I'd lost my commitment to the cause, but because I was exhausted. I felt like a soldier with post-traumatic stress disorder who wasn't allowed to leave the foxhole. Every day was a continuous barrage of incoming missiles and explosions, and I didn't have anywhere to go.

The way out appeared when a friend and former co-worker approached me about a position open where she worked. It was a position that would allow me to use the skills I'd learned and used at ACS CAN in an environment that had absolutely nothing to do with cancer. Would I be interested in exploring the possibility?

I was, albeit thinking honestly that this public health agency couldn't afford to hire me. And yet, after applying and having a great interview with the director and the deputy director of the agency, I got a job offer I knew I couldn't -- and wouldn't -- refuse.

As painful as it was to leave an organization into which I had poured my heart and soul, I knew my own mental and spiritual healing depended on my getting away and doing something different. I got calls from colleagues hoping they could talk me into staying, including a beautiful call from Molly Daniels, the deputy president of the organization. They wanted me to stay, but when I explained why it was imperative I go, they got it. They understood that it was time to go.

So I did. No regrets, no looking back.

I am now free to talk about cancer on my terms instead of being surrounded by talk of cancer 24 hours a day, seven days a week. I miss the people I worked with in the trenches, and I miss the volunteers who inspired me every day to do the work that I was doing, and I'm grateful every one of them understands why I had to leave.

Mindset Exercise

The process of letting go of negative experiences, things or people you believe are holding you back or states of emotion that are stifling your growth can be cathartic and freeing. Think carefully: What or whom in your life do you need to let go?

_____

_____

_____

Michael Holtz

Chapter 10 - Plan for Life After

"It's not an S. On my world, it means 'hope.' -- Superman

You never know when someone is going to come into your world and completely upend the life you've been living. My friend Zane is one of those people.

We "met" on Twitter, during the summer of 2010. I had followed him because while I didn't know him personally, I knew of him. Life in the world of advertising and public relations -- and everywhere else, I suppose -- is like that. We had even interacted a couple of times, ironically, now that I look back, joking about late nights and the colon-cleansing power of multiple pots of coffee.

One day I tweeted out a link to the Hotter 'n Hell 5K, an event I organized as a contingency fund-raiser for the American Cancer Society. He retweeted, saying it was a great event and a great cause. I knew from his Twitter bio that he was a runner and had once worked for The Wellness Community, precursor to the Cancer Support Community of East Tennessee. This was information I remembered when the Knoxville office began working to recruit athletes for the Society's now-defunct DetermiNation program. We wanted to get a group of area runners trained to run what was then the Country Music Marathon in Nashville.

Twitter was my only real connection to Zane, so I sent him a direct message asking whether he would be interested in talking about DetermiNation. He replied that he was and sent his mobile number. I know now that he almost never does that.

I called him. We talked briefly. We scheduled a meeting. From the outset it had all the appearances of a perfectly formal business relationship.

In person, he was clearly his own man. He wore blue jeans, a T-shirt and skull-and-crossbones Vans. His fingernails were painted black. His "you need me more than I need you" swagger, which I know makes some people think he is a complete asshole, was on full display.

I wondered what in the hell I had gotten myself into.

And then we started talking.

About the DetermiNation program to be sure, but more important, why he was interested. His dad, Charles, had passed away from cancer just a few years earlier, and Zane was a survivor himself. In his time at The Wellness Community, he'd had experience training groups of athletes to run and finish marathons. In fact, Zane was one of the founders of the Covenant Health Knoxville Marathon.

He said he wanted to help me. And he did.

We recruited 10 people to run the Country Music Marathon or Half-Marathon that year. A group of his clients/business associates had signed on, along with assorted friends. We trained, we ran the race, we raised somewhere in the neighborhood of $16,000.

For whatever reason, the man liked me and wanted to get more involved in the organization. His agency, z11 communications, sponsored and created the website for the Hotter 'n Hell 5K. He joined and briefly led the board's communications committee. He urged several of his clients to do fund-raisers for the Society, including a golf-swing improvement-tool company's effort to secure a world record for the number of golf swings made in a 24-hour period. And we recruited a smaller group of athletes to run the Rock 'n' Roll New Orleans Marathon for the DetermiNation program.

After the race, and not long after my diagnosis, we had a meeting in my office. I shared my news. There was this stony silence for a moment, and then Zane hugged me. There might have been a tear in his eye, but I'm not sure he will admit that. He did, though, want to keep up with my medical appointments and asked me to keep him in the loop. Over the next few weeks, as Sarah and I negotiated our way through scans and follow-up appointments, he wanted to know what was happening. If I didn't report, he would text me. This guy I barely knew, with whom I had a great rapport but only a business relationship to this point, wanted in his own way to be part of the most difficult journey I had ever faced.

Then came the unforgettable moment.

That Tuesday in the hospital, four days after the very difficult surgery, when the previously downcast surgeon came floating into my room on a cloud of happiness to report that the pathology report showed no living cancer cells. That day, when Sarah and I wept with gratitude with our dear, sweet pastor, who had been in the room with us to hear the good news. That day, Zane came to visit.

It wasn't long after Pastor Amy left. He strode into the room and perched himself on the window seat. I shared the news of the pathology report. There were definitely tears, from all of us. He will tell you he cried. It doesn't happen often.

I don't remember who else came to visit my hospital room that day, but I knew in that moment that I was not going to shake this guy. Zane was going to be, and is, an important part of my life. He has been one of my biggest supporters and an amazing source of encouragement in my life since cancer. He is a hero in his own right, and I love him like he's my brother by birth. We've had some great adventures together.

"We need a goal," is often how conversation -- either face-to-face or by text -- about our next adventure begins.

Our first goal was to do the Dopey Challenge at Walt Disney World in Orlando. The Dopey Challenge is four back-to-back days of races: 5K, 10K, half-marathon, marathon. That's 48.6 miles over four days. Zane paid for my entry, which carried a hefty price tag. It was my birthday present, he said.

It was March 2013. The race was 10 months away: theoretically, plenty of time to train and reclaim my body from the ravages of cancer treatment. Alas, it wasn't meant to be. Post-treatment fatigue, inflammation and neuropathy conspired to keep me from distance running, especially the neuropathy. It was difficult to try to train to run that kind of mileage when I could not feel the ground beneath my feet.

"We need a goal," he wrote in an email, which also included a link to a brand-new team mud-and-obstacle run. "I can't wait to see you do this with me."

It was intriguing. Mud and team obstacles on a 10K course through the wilderness.

"You know I can't run. I'm going to be so slow. And what if I shit on you?" I wrote back, worried I would have a colostomy appliance fail in the middle of the race.

His response back was something like "Just sign up already."

It was slow, probably excruciatingly so for him, but if he got impatient with me, he never let on. That day in May, we waded chest-deep in the fetid, algae-scum-covered water of a turtle pond. We bear-crawled up a hill. We tied ourselves together to do a three-legged hike up another hill. We rappelled into a ravine and climbed out.

Most impressively, for both of us, I carried him piggyback up a hill early in the race. Truth be told, he tried to pick me up, but his well-under-200-pound body wasn't going to pick up and carry a guy who weighed nearly twice as much. It wasn't happening. I didn't know whether I had the strength or energy to carry him, but we tried it anyway, and I succeeded in getting him up the hill.

We finished the race -- in last place, not that anyone but me was frustrated by that. And I missed only one obstacle, the last one, the Berlin Wall. Zane and a volunteer thought they could pull me over the wall, but I was exhausted, and after helping Zane get over, I was toast. Plus, the "race" part of the obstacle event turned out to be a little longer than organizers thought, by about two miles. I tapped the wall with my hand, and we headed toward the finish line.

Our adventures didn't end there, though.

Around the time of the obstacle race, I started working part time with Zane at his agency. He needed a writer, I like to write, so it seemed a natural fit. As part of my compensation, Zane paid for me to work out with him and his personal trainer, Brittney.

I was no stranger to personal training or strenuous workouts, but what Brittney concocted for us day after day was hard work involving military-style calisthenics, tire flips, sled pulls -- activities associated with either CrossFit or boot camp. It was hard work, but it was fun. And as I had gained back during treatment every one of the 100 pounds I'd lost before cancer, I needed to do something hard-core. This was definitely it.

We worked out in what was essentially a garage, what Brittney called "the dungeon," in a boutique gym on the north side of the city. The room was outfitted with all manner of tires, kettlebells, dumbbells, plyometric boxes, battle ropes, gymnastic rings and TRX straps.

Workouts were hard, and I was starting to see results. The number on the scale wasn't changing, but my body composition was.

A mutual acquaintance, Adam, joined our little group, and occasionally we would work outdoors on or around playground equipment. Outdoor workouts often involved a lot of running and bear crawls up the actual sides of hills. We worked out hard. Our bodies were changing for the better. I was stronger than I had ever been, even if I couldn't change the number on the scale.

One day I get a text from Zane.

"Can you meet us at Tennessee School of Beauty? Now."

Without question, I got up from my desk, got in my car and drove 10 minute to the destination. Zane and Adam were standing the empty shell of a warehouse space that had been previously occupied by a furniture-rental company. It was big and open, and dirty.

"We're going to open a gym," Zane said.

Brittney, who had also received the cryptic text message, arrived around the same time I did, and we looked at him, flabbergasted.

"We're what?" I asked.

"We're going to open a gym. You own a gym."

He went on to explain that he and Adam had been running together, training for a marathon, and had hatched the idea of taking this boot-camp exercise concept with a trainer we all liked a lot and sharing what Brittney does with a wider audience. Adam owned the space, he and Zane had agreed to buy the equipment, Brittney would be the trainer, and I would be the marketing and operations guy. I would be the CEO.

It was lunacy, and yet it was the best idea ever. What none of them knew was this: before cancer, when I was healthy and in the best shape of my life, I'd wanted to become a personal trainer and help other people find the healthiness and happiness that I'd found. This group was about to help make that dream come true.

We opened the doors of Adaptive Fitness Warehouse on October 1, 2013. We called ourselves that because any workout Brittney created could be adapted to meet the needs of each individual taking part, regardless of illness, injury or fitness level. In short order, we created what was, in essence, another tribe. Through Brittney's fitness contacts, Zane's business clients and friends, Adam's students at the beauty school he owned, and through marketing, we built a small but mighty community of people dedicated to getting themselves healthy.

One of my favorite moments at AFW happened that Thanksgiving, during a special holiday workout Brittney designed to torch about 2,000 calories for anyone who completed it. It was perfect for a holiday where people were going to load up on rich, fattening foods. All of us were finished working out, but one person, NeNe, was on the floor doing her last set of rampages, and she was struggling. To a person, we all stopped what we were doing, dropped to the floor and counted out the last set with her. No man or woman left behind.

The most fun I ever had at Adaptive Fitness Warehouse, though, took place during the summer at our outdoor boot camps. We would meet at 6 a.m. and spend 90 minutes doing whatever Brittney conceived for us that day: suicide sprints up and down the soccer field, sled pushes, bear crawls, you name it.

And I loved working out with the people in our boot camp: Zane, Scarlet, Jeff, Christie, Tiffany, Erin, Meghan, Lynn and Lauren. During every workout together, we laughed and cut up, and we worked hard, and we supported each other. Jeff would later say that no matter what emotions he brought with him to the workout, he always left in a better mood. It was the people who made that happen. I agree wholeheartedly.

A community of support, where people are not defined by weight or body shape or ability: we built that that Adaptive Fitness Warehouse. It was an amazing place and also remains a bit of a dream. We have decided to change our business model and become a nonprofit organization, with the intent of taking our gym to the underserved parts of our community. There are places in Knoxville, as in many communities across the country, where lack of access to nutritious food combined with lack of easy access to physical activity conspire to increase obesity and, therefore, risk factors for heart disease, stroke, diabetes and cancer. Unfortunately, we did not get approval from the Internal Revenue Service for our nonprofit organization, so -- for now, anyway -- the dream is on hold.

Zane and I have a favorite adventure so far: it's the day we jumped into the icy Tennessee River in January as part of a fund-raiser for Big Brothers Big Sisters of East Tennessee.

We saw a banner for the Penguin Plunge at one of our favorite watering holes. As one is wont to do when judiciously lubricated, we agreed to sign up to "take the plunge." Naturally, it was easier said than done. The day of the big event, on the first Saturday of the New Year, the air temperature was somewhere around 15 degrees, which meant the water temperature would be in the neighborhood of "brisk."

Because Zane knows everybody (and I know everybody else), we managed to make our way onto the dock with a group from the event's presenting sponsor -- that watering hole I mentioned earlier. We were going to be first in and first out of the water.

Now, I have to tell you that Sarah was a bit worried about me making this jump. There are horror stories from similar events where the hearts of large, overweight people go into shock and stop because of the frigid temperatures. And what if the neuropathy kicked in really badly and I couldn't make it back to the dock.

"Zane will be right beside me," I said. "And there are EMTs on standby. Worst-case scenario: my colostomy bag falls off in the water." That sucker was held in place with waterproof tape and a belt, so it wasn't going anywhere.

As it turns out, everything was fine -- very, very cold, but absolutely fine. We jumped in, paddled back to the dock and climbed out. We quickly changed clothes, got warm beverages and headed on to the rest of our respective days.

I have a preplunge photo of us in my office. It's a great picture.

Our conversation about adventures took a turn for the big and audacious last spring when, over a couple beers (naturally), Zane mentioned that he has always dreamed of running with the bulls in Pamplona.

Thing is, I had harbored a similar dream since reading Ernest Hemingway's *The Sun Also Rises* in high school.

"I need to become a much faster runner," I said.

"And you need to build up your strength. You'll have to carry me after I get gored in the side," he said.

That's what he said. He wants a scar that shows he's been gored by a bull. Random, and a wee bit crazy, and I would follow him anywhere.

That conversation led me to create a bucket list, my list of things I would like to do in my post-cancer life. I posted the original list on my old blog, Outrunning Cancer, but I've made a few tweaks and modifications. Here, then, is my list:

- Sing a role onstage in *Les Miserables* (any production, any role)
- Write my own book
- Go on a book tour
- Learn to play guitar (at last!)
- Visit Antarctica
- Bike tour of the Florida Keys
- Spend a week in silence
- Vacation on Mackinac Island
- Give inspirational/motivational speech to a ballroom full of people (COMPLETED July 14, 2014)
- Help develop an environmentally friendly pouching system
- Be in a clinical trial for use of laboratory-grown rectal tissue
- Skydive
- Hot-air balloon
- Lose enough weight to be able to do #12 and #13
- Go to seminary
- Run with the bulls in Pamplona
- Get out of debt
- Buy a larger house
- Become foster parents
- Own a Land Rover (specifically, an Evoque)
- Get an audience with Pope Francis
- Shake the president's hand
- Have a dish named after me
- Cook with Tyler Florence
- Swim with Michael Phelps
- Visit Paris
- Throw out a first pitch

- Help make an ill child's wish come true
- Participate in the Empire State Building Run-Up
- Run in New Year's Eve Midnight Run in Central Park
- Donate books for cancer patients
- Have dinner with Bruce Willis
- Meet the CEO of Exact Sciences, a company that is changing the world (COMPLETED July 14, 2014)
- Get a tattoo (COMPLETED June 2014)
- Bungee jump from a bridge in Mexico
- Learn Spanish (useful for both #16 and #36 and possibly #22)
- Appear in The Colon Club's Colondar
- Run the Covenant Health Knoxville Marathon in 5:15
- Become a personal trainer
- Get my ear pierced
- Run a sub-30-minute 5K
- Meet Ann Voskamp, author of *one thousand gifts* (COMPLETED December 12, 2014)

Clearly, I still have a lot to accomplish, but the items that have been completed were amazing moments. I gave a motivational speech to the National Sales Meeting at Exact Sciences Corporation, the company that developed Cologuard, the easiest-ever screening test for colorectal cancer, after their social-media staffer saw a post about my bucket list on Twitter. At that event, I got to meet Kevin Conroy, the company's CEO. I am grateful to him for writing the foreword to this book.

Zane has mentored other motivational speakers and helped me immensely in shaping the speech I gave that night. He knew, because he had heard the words that I was going to talk about him during the presentation -- about the importance of having an encourager and supporter to keep you motivated and excited about life after cancer. He knew I was going to refer to him as one of my heroes. I mean, in addition to being an amazing friend and a freaking genius with the unfortunate social skills of Sheldon Cooper, the man ran 26 marathons in 2014, nine of them back to back. Sometimes I feel unworthy to unlace his running shoes.

But I know the hero thing is mutual. "You're one of my heroes too," he texted five minutes before I took the stage in Madison.

This book was actually borne from that presentation. While I had been planning to write a book about my cancer experience, I really had not come up with a way to present my story. My presentation that night was about five things I learned during my cancer journey. The mindsets in this book are an expansion of that idea. He built my website, michaelholtzonline.com, which will serve as a platform for my blog, this and future books, and what I hope will become a robust motivational-speaking career.

That Spain thing is still out there too, if we can stop long enough from our insanely busy lives to plan the trip and get there for what has to be an amazing week in July. As cancer survivors, we both understand that life is tenuous and there is much to be celebrated every day. There is still a lot of living to do.

Zane, we need a goal.

Mindset Exercise

Creating a bucket list is a great way to set goals for your life during and after cancer treatment or other serious illness. If you could do anything, go anywhere, meet anyone, what would you do? Think big, and then make plans to cross items off your list.

_____

_____

_____

_____

_____

Chapter 11 - Give Back

"Hardships often prepare ordinary people for an extraordinary destiny." -- C.S. Lewis

I never met David, but I'll never forget the impact he had on my life. Between February and July of 2014, I was his "Chemo Angel."

Chemo Angels is an amazing nonprofit organization that matches caring people with individuals undergoing intravenous chemotherapy treatment. Angels provide support in the form of cards and small gifts mailed weekly to their assigned patient.

I learned about Chemo Angels from my friend Belinda (Bart from the Cancer Support Community art class). She had a Chemo Angel and raved about the gifts and notes she was getting from a woman halfway across the country whom she didn't even know.

After my own experience, and as a means of acknowledging the reality that not everyone has the system of support in place that I did, I signed up to be a Chemo Angel for someone.

That's how I got connected with David in February.

The folks at Angel headquarters do an amazing job of filling volunteers in with details about their assigned patients. I knew David was from New York State, was married, and had kids. He was being treated for esophageal cancer. He liked nuts, coffee, chocolate, '80s rock, football and the smell of citrus, and he loved his family.

Every week during those six months, I kept a lookout for gifts I could send to David. I was traveling a lot both personally and for work, so my gifts often came from travel destinations: a pen from Washington, D.C., a keychain from the Great Smoky Mountains National Park, coffee from a great shop in Annapolis. For Easter, I sent his kids a basket overflowing with candy and other fun items.

I wrote a note with each gift too. I let David know I was praying for him and his family and that I hoped he was doing well under the rigors of chemo, but that was it for the cancer talk. I remember from my own experience how much

I appreciated normal, noncancer conversation, so I held to that in my correspondence with David. I talked about my travels for work, or what Sarah and I had planned for the next weekend, or some funny thing our dog did -- light and conversational, and I hope a distraction from any pain or discomfort caused by treatment.

Even though I didn't know him, I understood what he was going through.

Were about the same age. We liked a lot of the same things. While I had never seen his picture, I visualized him undergoing chemo. I could picture him, remembering myself and those around me from when I was in the chemo chair. I prayed over every package I sent off to him.

I didn't know David, yet I loved him. And he loved getting my packages.

I know because I would get a note from an administrator at Chemo Angels, who forwarded messages from David.

This came in April:

"I am doing as well as can be. My treatments are going as planned, and I will be getting a follow-up CT scan on Monday to see how well the chemotherapy is working. I would like my angels to know that no matter how bad a day I'm having, something seems to show up in my mailbox just to let me know they are thinking about me. I think that this program is amazing for people who are going through the fight. To know a total stranger is taking time out of their life just to send a card or something else is so supportive."

By July, his situation had changed:

"It seems as though my current chemo is not working. It was shrinking the tumor in my esophagus, but they recently found cancer cells in the fluid in my lung lining. My oncologist told me there is a new single agent approved for esophageal cancer, so I will probably be put on that next. I will find out soon as I am currently hospitalized for blood clots in my lungs, pneumonia and pleural effusions. I really appreciate both my angels and have come to really look forward to receiving their thoughtful words. Please tell them that I always want to send thank-you cards to let them know that I truly appreciate them, but I always find myself feeling horrible and just trying to spend time with my two young boys. I am very happy with both of my angels, and I thank you again for this organization. It means a lot to me."

His birthday was July 25. Given the challenge he was facing with treatment, I wanted to do something big, something more than a small package of some random gift I picked up at the airport on my way to or from a plane. I decided to send him a balloon bouquet.

Online, I found a floral shop in his hometown and placed an order for the bouquet to be delivered on the afternoon before his birthday. On the day it was delivered, the floral shop sent a confirmation email. Three weeks later, I learned that David died on the very day those balloons were delivered.

Of course, I was sad David had died, and I was mortified at the horrible timing of a "Happy Birthday" balloon bouquet arriving at the home of a dead man. I imagined his wife thought me a cold, heartless person, but she didn't.

This is the message from his family:

"I would like to thank you for your care and concern and for being so proactive in trying to make those who fight cancer and deal with chemo feel a little more cared about. It is a wonderful service you provide. His Chemo Angels cheered him up on many occasions. Thank them also for him."

The administrative folks at Chemo Angels asked if I wanted to re-up and take on another Angel assignment. I declined temporarily, to give myself the time and space to recover from losing a friend I never met.

Death is part of the whole cancer thing. We fear it when we're diagnosed, we acknowledge its possibility throughout the course of treatment, and we taunt it when our cancer experience ends well. Not everyone gets the opportunity to taunt death on the other side of their cancer journey. David certainly didn't.

A friend I care about very much recently finished his cancer treatment and, I am happy to say, got an all clear from his doctors. While we have celebrated the end of his treatment, there were days I know it wasn't easy for him. I worried I was going to say goodbye to another friend battling this horrible disease. I know he didn't want me worrying, but that couldn't be helped. It's part of the deal.

I thought about that the day I requested a new Chemo Angel assignment. I'm now Angel Michael to a patient in Pittsburgh. I know it's unlikely I will ever meet him, but that doesn't matter. While I'm alive, I want to give back what I have while I can. A few bucks and a few minutes a week to buy a trinket and write a note that will surely brighten a cancer patient's day: I've got time for that, and it's a great way to give back using what I learned through my own experience.

I also give back using my long-distance running and walking experience. My friend Anthony Palmer invited me to be the walking coach for the Leukemia and Lymphoma Society Team in Training program during the fall 2013 training season. Anthony and I met while he was an intern at the Knoxville Track Club, where I volunteered for all those race events I mentioned earlier.

As walk coach, my responsibility was to help folks planning to walk a half-marathon to be trained and ready to finish their event. It may sound like the focus is on training, but the truth is that Team in Training is a fund-raiser with a training component attached. Still, the training is important in helping athletes prepare for their chosen events. The run coach and I developed a training schedule, and for about three months every season we helped folks committed to the cause prepare for their events. I was a coach for two seasons, and I absolutely loved meeting the athletes and program coaches from the running and triathlon programs.

I hope to return to coaching one day, but I had to give it up so I could pursue the dream of a faster marathon of my own. Yes, I wrote in the introduction that I would never run another marathon for the rest of my days. The right person asked at the right time and for the right cause, so as I write this I'm training for the Covenant Health Knoxville Marathon. I'm hoping to finish in 5:15 but I really just want to cross the finish line.

Other ways I give back include participating in local Relay For Life events, only now I get to participate as just myself, not as a former employee.

Relay For Life, as you may know, is the American Cancer Society's signature fund-raising event. As I have mentioned, I worked there, so I could give you in detail the history of this event, but I'll save that for them. Suffice it to say that a doctor in Tacoma, Washington, wanted to do something to raise money for the Society, so he ran around a high school track for 24 hours in 1985. Thus was born what is now the largest fund-raising event in the world.

My Relay For Life is held at Knoxville's World's Fair Park every year. Every event begins with a celebration of cancer survivors, who together walk the first lap of the Relay. Now, I've been a Relay For Life participant for years, even before I went to work for the Society. Walking that lap for the first time with other survivors and being cheered on by my community -- I still get goose bumps just thinking about it.

Relay, by the way, is a great way to find your tribe, especially if there isn't access to a cancer support group or other service. So many of my tribe members have come from my Relay experiences. I knew a lot of survivors as a natural part of doing Society business, but when I crossed over and became one myself, those relationships changed. I was no longer writing about cancer survivorship from a theoretical or third-person perspective. As was the case with my cancer-patient support group, I understood what it meant to be a survivor. I had the battle scars to prove it.

Another event in which I participate is one my community lovingly refers to as "Buddy's Race."

Buddy's Race Against Cancer is an experience similar to but very different from Relay for Life. There is a survivor celebration component, but there is a much larger community presence. Thousands of people run in Buddy's Race, which was named for Buddy Smothers, the founder of Buddy's BBQ, a local chain. Buddy's Race raises money for the nonprofit foundation at Thompson Cancer Survival Center, where I was treated. The foundation uses the money to fund cancer-screening outreach programs for people who could not otherwise afford to get screened.

Buddy's really is a race. Something like 5,000 people turn out to run the 5K, or walk, or take a walk around World's Fair Park. The race is a great opportunity to connect or reconnect with survivors I know: hoards of my running friends participate, and there are lots of folks from the cancer center itself. Because of all of that, Buddy's Race is one of my favorite events of the year. I absolutely love it and have recruited a team to participate every year since my diagnosis.

Honestly, I believe that because I am alive, I have a duty to give back to organizations that fight cancer. Selfishly, it feels good. Altruistically, other people get the help they need. When you think about it, giving back is easy.

Mindset Exercise

How do you see yourself giving back to others, whether to a cancer-fighting organization or to another cause close to your heart? What does that look like for you?

_____

_____

_____

Chapter 12: Stay Vigilant

"Health is the greatest gift, contentment the greatest wealth, faithfulness the greatest relationship." – The Buddha

As it turns out, my doctors did not tell me everything there was to know about my cancer in those early, frightening days between diagnosis and plan of attack. If they had, I'm not sure I would have that much to write about. Fear and self-pity over the severity of my illness might have sent me down a different path.

My diagnosis was Stage-3b rectal cancer, which meant there was a three-inch undifferentiated adenocarcinoma attached to the wall of my rectum, and there was cancer in a handful of lymph nodes -- three to be exact -- but the cancer had not metastasized. If I had waited a bit longer to see my primary-care doctor when I saw blood in the toilet, someone else might be telling my story.

"There was cancer in the capsule of your lymph nodes," Dr. Liebman, my oncologist, told us about halfway through my chemotherapy schedule. "Given a little more time, the cancer would have broken through the capsule and gotten into your bloodstream."

A little more time? How long? A week? Two? A month?

Dr. Liebman couldn't tell us for sure. All that mattered was that we caught the cancer in time to do something about it.

The thought of a close call gave us pause. I knew vigilance about my health was important, never more so than knowing I was possibly days from a Stage-4 diagnosis. But there was more.

"You're not supposed to be this healthy," Dr. Midis said during my two-year postsurgery follow-up appointment. "You should not be standing here. I hope you appreciate how lucky you are."

I didn't know what to say.

I mean, I have long known that my risk of recurrence is very high. During the first two years after diagnosis, there was an 80 percent chance of recurrence. Now my risk hovers around 70 percent.

Because of that, Dr. Midis wants to keep a close watch on me.

I will see him every four to six months for a CEA test, the test that indicates colorectal-cancer activity in my bloodstream, and once a year get a PET or CT scan.

"If you notice any changes, you call my office immediately. We have to stay on top of this."

Odd thing is, since my treatment ended, I've seen recurrence as an inevitability. I'm not afraid of cancer's return. I've faced it once; I'll face it again. And everything I've written about in this book will continue to be true.

Still, I am vigilant about my health.

I pay close attention to the operation of my digestive system and what gets expelled into my colostomy bags.

I am working on losing the weight I regained during cancer treatment. It's a challenge I know all too well. When I lament about how much more difficult it is to lose weight this time around, I have to remember that I'm older, I've been through hell -- and, oh yeah, there was a tumor in my ass when I was at my smallest. I still get frustrated, though.

I exercise regularly. I watch what I eat. I set challenging fitness goals for myself. I need a goal to keep me focused. If I'm working toward something -- a speed goal, a marathon, whatever -- I'm better at keeping focused on my nutrition and physical-activity goals.

I ran into Dr. Midis a few minutes after I crossed the finish line at this year's Buddy's Race. I was wearing a Superman shirt. To my surgeon, it was a wholly appropriate shirt.

"Superman. That's a perfect shirt for you to be wearing," Dr. Midis said, as he smiled and shook my hand. "Very appropriate indeed. You clearly look like you're feeling good."

"I'm feeling great," I said. "If that changes, I promise I'll be in touch."

This probably falls more in the category of giving back, but it's also appropriate from a vigilance perspective. I have been asked to be the lead volunteer from my congressional district for my former employer, the American Cancer Society Cancer Action Network. In that capacity, I will be in regular touch with the office of U.S. Representative John J. Duncan Jr. about the importance of funding cancer research and prevention programs, as well as any other issues that rise to the top of ACS CAN's legislative agenda. Fortunately, after years as an ACS CAN staff member, I have a good relationship with my congressman.

I have also been vigilant about cancer research, especially funding for research. I have served and will serve again as an advocate reviewer for both the Cancer Research and Prevention Institute of Texas and the Department of Defense Congressionally Directed Medical Research Program. As an advocate reviewer, I represent the voice of colorectal-cancer patients in discussions among scientists about research proposals being considered for funding. It is an honor, a privilege and an enormous responsibility to serve in this role, and I am grateful to the Colon Cancer Alliance for asking me to serve in this capacity. I have learned a lot, including the fact that there is a whole lot of research being proposed to eradicate cancers. There is hope for a cure one day.

Finally, my vigilance includes sharing my story. There is this book, of course, but I also share what I experienced and what I've learned on my blog, with individuals and to groups. I believe that as a survivor, I have a responsibility to demystify the colorectal-cancer treatment experience and to share what I've learned about myself and about life during treatment. What I know and what I learned boils down to this: cancer sucks, and treating it can be difficult, but with the right attitude and with great people by your side, cancer can be faced bravely and with determination.

I know because I've been there.

Mindset Exercise

You were diagnosed with a disease, you fought it with the best medicine mankind has to offer so far, and you've survived. Like being hounded by wolves, you will think about recurrence, which is a possibility. You'll have to stay vigilant by doing things like keeping your follow-up doctor appointments, getting healthy, losing weight, eating better. Make a commitment to yourself, your family and to your health. What will you do to stay vigilant?

_____

_____

_____

Michael Holtz

About the Author

Michael Holtz is a thriver, a word he prefers over "survivor" of Stage-3b rectal cancer. He has embraced the second chance he was given by sharing the life lessons he learned during his cancer journey. He lives in Knoxville, Tenn., with the lovely Sarah, and their rescue dog, a Golden Bassett named Marley. Michael and Sarah have a great life filled with love and support from their friends and family.

Michael is a long-time public relations and marketing practitioner, currently plying his trade as a part-time account coordinator for z11 communications. He also works as the Director of Community Assessment and Health Promotion for the Knox County Health Department. He holds a bachelor's degree in mass communication from the University of Wisconsin-Milwaukee, a master's degree in communications from the University of Tennessee, and he is accredited in public relations by the Universal Accreditation Board and the Public Relations Society of America.

He can be reached through his website, www.michaelholtzonline.com, on Facebook @MichaelAndrewHoltz and on Twitter @michaelholtz.

54428967R00116

Made in the USA
Charleston, SC
01 April 2016